Maximizing
Your
Effectiveness

By Aubrey Malphurs

*Developing a Vision for Ministry
in the 21st Century*

*Planting Growing Churches
for the 21st Century*

*Pouring New Wine
into Old Wineskins*

Vision America

Maximizing
Your
Effectiveness

*How to Discover and Develop
Your Divine Design*

Aubrey Malphurs

Foreword by Carl George

Baker Books
A Division of Baker Book House Co
Grand Rapids, Michigan 49516

© 1995 by Aubrey Malphurs

Published by Baker Books
a division of Baker Book House Company
P.O. 6287, Grand Rapids, MI 49516-6287

Second printing, June 1997

Printed in the United States of America

Library of Congress Cataloging-in-Publication Data

Malphurs, Aubrey.
    Maximizing your effectiveness : how to discover and develop your divine design /
Aubrey Malphurs.
      p.   cm.
    Includes bibliographical references and index.
    ISBN 0-8010-6317-5
    1. Clergy—Office. 2. Pastoral theology. I. Title.
BV660.2.M251995
253—dc20   94-40064

For current information about all releases from Baker Book House,
visit our web site:
http://www.bakerbooks.com

To my friend Bruce L. Bugbee
who first catalyzed my thinking
in the area of creative design.
May his tribe increase.

Contents

Foreword

The three dominant generations of Americans who now play significant roles in the general society are all in need of guidance. The Sponsor generation must deal with the consequences of an unprecedented longevity. The Boomers are hit with the digital revolution and its resulting corporate downsizing and job dislocations. The rising Generation X faces a world in which their elders can barely cope, much less give counsel, struggling as they are to find direction themselves as they experience collapses of familiar paradigms in almost every field of endeavor. There is a widely felt cry for personal reevaluation.

Increasingly, the restless and unending search for personal meaning that characterizes much of contemporary life reaches throughout society and into the church.

An industry, the self-help publishing sector, is arising to address the questions: Of what am I capable? What is my potential? Why am I here? What is to become of me? Is there a meaning and purpose for my life? How do I find fulfillment? At what kinds of activities will I be good? How can I make a contribution to the lives of others? How can I make the most of my talents and opportunities?

The devout Christian adds these questions: What does God expect of me? What clues to God's call are to be found in understanding how God has made me? How can I cooperate with the Creator to bring his plans for me and the world into existence?

This book is a manual for coming to understand yourself and what you should do with yourself. It lays out a process for thinking through the questions that gives practical, straightforward guidance to those who will take the time to work patiently through it. And it makes use of the spiritual-gift discovery and personality-type indentification tools that have proved to be so helpful in churches over the past two decades.

The prayerful Christian, willing to listen as well as ask, will be challenged by the awesome implications of realizing what stewardship of a life can mean, in terms of personal fulfillment as well as benefit to humankind. Dr. Malphurs's work in *Maximizing Your Effectiveness* helpfully marks a path to that realization.

—Carl George

Introduction

Carol was excited about her new church and the authentic ministry it had in her life. She and her husband had grown up Baptist in south Texas where church was a way of life—where it had become deeply embedded in their bones. But he was transferred, and now they found themselves in another part of the country attending a new, intentionally different church. She was told that the rapidly growing church had been planted five years ago as a "new paradigm" church—whatever that meant. Regardless, the pastor's sermons had a profound impact on her life. She had heard the Bible preached before but not with such integrity, vulnerability, and relevance.

Most of all, she was amazed at the number of passionate people her age who were involved "up to their elbows" in one form of ministry or another. The tiny congregation in the little church back home had always insisted that the ministry was the pastor's job, not theirs—that is what they paid him for! She could remember being coaxed into teaching a class of bored adolescents and hating every minute of it. When she resigned a year later, she swore she would never be abused like that again. She almost left the church. But this situation was entirely different. It seemed as if all her friends were somehow involved in significant ministry and loving every minute of it. They called it authentic ministry: They were doing what God had designed them to do. But what could she do? Where could she serve? Would it be another miserable experience? And how might she discover the answers to these and other similar questions?

Lately Tom had trouble falling asleep. Once he was securely under the covers, he tossed and turned much of the night. And when he did fall asleep, a passing car or the neighbor's barking dog easily awakened him. This was highly unusual. In the past, once his head contacted the pillow, he remembered absolutely nothing until his faithful alarm awakened him early the next morning. But life was different now; it had taken a new twist.

Two years before, Tom had come to faith in the Savior through the ministry of Campus Crusade for Christ. Another student, who sat next to him in English 101, had periodically invited him to informal get-togethers in the dorm. Finally, when he told Tom that the attractive young lady seated behind them would be there, Tom took the bait. That night Tom heard the claims of Christ, and things had not been the same since. While he had grown up in a church, spiritual things had never made much sense until that special night when they all came together. While it had not been a deeply moving experience—he was not an emotional guy—he did feel a tear welling up in the corner of his eye as he embraced the Savior.

After that night, life quickly took on a whole new perspective. It was as if Tom had finally found what he had been looking for. A missing piece of life's puzzle had fallen into place. He quietly sensed that things would be different from here on. It was both a little frightening and exciting. One of the Crusade directors noted Tom's abilities and saw much potential for Christ. He pulled Tom alongside and began to nurture his newfound faith.

Now two years later, graduation was just around the corner, and Tom was struggling with life after college. Should he pursue what looked to be a decent future in the marketplace? He could return to his blue-collar roots and go home to run his dad's gas station for a while. Or he could pursue vocational Christian ministry. What should he do with the rest of his life, and how could he discern which was the best choice for him in his circumstances? Would he make a good businessman, station manager, or pastor? Where could he best glorify his Savior? Which pursuit would best use the gifts, talents, and abilities that God had given him? Chances were good he would not experience another good night's sleep until he resolved these questions.

Like Tom, David had his share of insomnia. But their situations were different. David was a Christian who had graduated from seminary, married his college sweetheart, and had been a pastor for the last two years—two years that he would describe as the most difficult years of his life.

When he originally applied to the seminary, the application inquired about his vocational plans. He did not have a clue. Initially, as a growing, committed Christian, he wanted to know more about the Bible and theology, so he put that down. That response must have been okay because a month later he received his acceptance in the mail. Toward the end of seminary he chose the pastoral track because one or two of his influential friends had done the same, and he was under pressure—he had to make a decision or delay the completion of his last year.

Upon graduation he and his new bride accepted a call to a small church in a sleepy little town not far from where her parents lived. That is where the nightmare began. The first year was tolerable. He spent most of his time in his study doing what he liked best: studying and preparing scholarly sermons and messages for Sunday morning, Sunday evening, and Wednesday night prayer meeting. What he did not like was the interruptions: weddings, funerals, and pastoral visitation.

In time the criticism began to mount like a tidal wave bearing down on a solitary bather on some lonely beach. The most vocal complaint related to his people skills: "Our pastor should have been a teacher, not a preacher. He loves his books more than his people!" Ouch! That hurt! But deep down in his heart, he knew they were right. He did not seem to fit. What he was doing—pastoral ministry—was not authentic. What should he do? What could he do? Had he made the wrong choice in seminary? Should he leave the church and find another church? Should he even stay in the ministry? Should he pursue doctoral studies? These questions and others recycled through his mind at bedtime and often would not allow him to fall asleep.

Carol, Tom, and David represent the future of the church of Jesus Christ in America and abroad. And it promises to be a delightful future because all, in different contexts, have a deep, God-given desire to serve their Savior in some significant ministry. But they are not sure how to go about it. Everywhere the questions are the same: How can I best serve the risen Savior either as a lay person in my church or as a full-time person in a vocational ministry? How can I serve God authentically, that is, with the feeling that who he has made me to be connects with what I am doing? I am convinced that believers will not experience the joy and satisfaction of authentic ministry until they are serving Christ in ministries consistent with how God designed them: with their spiritual gifts, passions, temperaments, talents, abilities, and leadership styles.

The problem lies in the answer, or better the lack of an answer. Committed Christian people desire to discover their true place in the body of Christ but are not sure how to go about it. Is the answer found in playing some kind of guessing game with God? Is serious involvement in Christian ministry a trial-and-error process? Does it involve one in a simple cast of the divine die, or is it some kind of colossal, cosmic crapshoot?

I have written this book to help serious Christians like Carol, Tom, and David find some answers to their questions, and in turn to discover their places of service in Christ's body whether part- or full-time. Ultimately what they are seeking is a ministry direction—their personal ministry vision. Life for the believer does not have to be unfulfilled, meaningless, without purpose. Instead Christ offers meaning and significance in his service. The key is discovering your personal ministry vision—your ministry niche. And the result is authentic ministry.

Our vision for ministry exists both on a personal and institutional level. Institutional vision relates directly to the ministry of a particular Christian organization whether church or parachurch. I wrote *Developing a Vision for Ministry in the 21st Century* to help leaders develop unique institutional visions tailor-made for the organizations they lead or are a part of. *Maximizing Your Effectiveness: How to Discover and Develop Your Divine Design* is the companion volume designed to help individuals discover their personal ministry visions. Once Christians have determined their personal visions, they would be wise to identify with a ministry organization that has an organizational vision aligning itself most closely with their personal ministry visions. This prevents ministry burnout and in time achieves a greater impact because it has the entire ministry organization behind it.

Several churches in America have become pioneers in developing programs to help their congregations discover their personal ministry visions. Bruce Bugbee gave birth to the well-designed Networking program for the people at Willow Creek Community Church located in northwest suburban Chicago, and it has served them well. The same is true of Pastor Rick Warren who has implemented the exciting SHAPE program at Saddleback Church in Mission Viejo, California. In addition, several ministry assessment centers now exist in various parts of the country to help those considering full-time ministry, especially church planters, determine their ministry visions. Though Willow Creek and Saddleback are large, influential churches, it is doubtful that Carol, Tom, David, and most of America will be helped by their ministries. And as helpful as professional assessment centers may be, most people, especially lay people, will not likely seek out their valuable services.

   This book is designed precisely for these people. Discovering our place in the body of Christ is a process consisting of three distinct phases that relate directly to the three parts of this book. Part 1, "Discovering Your Personal Design for Ministry," is the logical starting place. It focuses on your ministry design and answers the question, Who are you?

   Part 1 consists of four chapters that will help Christians understand how God has uniquely designed them for spiritual service inside or outside the walls of the church. Chapter 1 introduces the biblical concept of divine design by showing from Scripture how God has uniquely crafted and equipped each of us for ministry within his divine purpose and plan. Chapter 2 emphasizes the importance of discovering that design, which results in knowing who you are, liking who you are, and being who you are. Chapter 3 presents the different components that make up the Christian's design, such as spiritual gifts, passion, temperament, natural talents and abilities, and leadership style. Chapter 4 presents and applies the various tools available to assist in the process of discerning our unique, divine design.

   Part 2, "Determining Your Personal Vision for Ministry," builds on Part 1 and addresses the primary question of the book, What can I do? Once people know and understand their ministry design, the next step is to discover their ministry direction—their personal ministry vision. Part 2 consists of two chapters. Chapter 5 explains the biblical concept that God has a unique, fulfilling place of ministry for each person in the body of Christ. Chapter 6 leads you through the process of determining your unique, ministry niche.

   Part 3, "Directing Your Personal Development for Ministry," presents the third logical step in the process. Once we know our ministry design and ministry direction, we need to answer the question of ministry development: How do I prepare for my ministry vision? What is the best plan, considering my design, to help me best accomplish my direction? Chapter 7 focuses on the concept and contents of a plan, and chapter 8 assists you in the development of a training plan unique to your ministry.

   The discovery of personal and organizational ministry vision helps Christians in general and leaders in particular to determine their future place of ministry in the body of Christ. Consequently this book and its companion are for all serious Christians whether on a lay or professional level who desire to be called God's servants. I suspect that this describes you, or you would not have read this far. I suggest you read this book with

your Christian friends and the people in your church or parachurch ministry. Be sure to discuss it with them because their insight into your life will
be of great value to you. After you have read it and understand your personal vision for ministry, then read *Developing a Vision for Ministry in the
21st Century* to determine your organizational vision for the ministry you
lead or are a part of. Then answer the question, Am I serving in a ministry
organization that best uses my ministry design and vision?

Part 1

Discovering Your
Personal Design
for Ministry

The first part of this book is aimed at helping you understand that God has designed you in a wonderful, unique way for service in the body of Christ. Further, it will help you understand what your divine design is. This is a necessary prerequisite to determining your ministry vision. Who you are is as important as what you do. Design for ministry precedes direction of ministry.

The key to determining what you can do in the body of Christ is discovering who you are—your ministry identity in Christ.

The Concept of
Your Divine Design

1

Who Do You Think You Are?

Most people have a profound inner desire to accomplish something of importance with their lives during their brief stay on planet Earth. They want more than anything to lead fulfilling, productive lives that leave them with a deep sense of significance. The reality is that few, very few, will achieve it, and most do not know what it is. Consultants Mattson and Miller say, "Somewhere between 50 to 80 percent of working Americans occupy jobs wrong for them, according to published surveys."[1] They provide several examples:

> In the teaching profession, we have found that at least two-thirds are not motivated to teach, and we have been criticized for being conservative in our estimates. Examining managers and executives, we have found that only one out of three appears well-matched to his job. Many clergy are not gifted at central requirements like preaching, teaching, and evangelism. One wonders how bad it is with waitresses, doctors, bankers, electricians, and assembly workers.[2]

Unfortunately this is true of far too many who make up the Christian community. Many do not know who they are, why they are here, and what they are supposed to accomplish with their lives. The result is nominal

Christianity. Few Christians seem fulfilled and lead what they believe to be happy, productive lives for Christ. Instead many go through this life with a sense of having missed something, of having never realized their full potential for the kingdom of God.

Major culprits are the secular models of human behavior. Public schools, colleges and universities, even the media, mirror these secular concepts so that the average Christian unknowingly imbibes them on a regular basis. The result is much confusion among Christians and a misunderstanding of how God has designed them. But what are these secular models, and more important, what does the Bible have to say about people and their design? Just who do you think you are?

Two Models of Human Nature

While several models of the nature of man have surfaced over the centuries, two have affected the Christian mind in particular.[3] These two views are polar opposites that have exerted a major influence on how people in general and Christians in particular view themselves and their roles and potential for accomplishment in this life.[4]

The Deterministic Model

Students of behavior who promote the deterministic or mechanistic model believe a person is born into this world as a piece of clay or a blank slate. Various forces in the environment, such as parents, teachers, peers, and the workplace, act as potters or scribes to mold and shape or write upon the person and, in essence, determine to a large extent who he or she is. The point is that persons become who they are in response to and under the primary influence of others. The behavioral perspective that undergirds this model had its origin in the middle of the twentieth century and was influenced by the work of men such as B. F. Skinner. Though modified to some degree, it continues up to the present and exerts an enormous impact on the psychological world.[5]

A major problem is that this model strips individuals of any personal responsibility for their actions. When a person sins or even commits some heinous crime against society, mechanists are quick to rally around that person and argue that he or she is not to blame for that behavior. They argue that, instead, society in general or the individual's immediate environment is to blame. The person is simply mirroring society in all its ugliness and injustice. The person must not be made to pay for the crime; rather, society is ultimately paying for its crimes against humanity.

Like so many other ideas bantered about in this world, this view of man has some merit. Little question exists that people are affected by their environment, especially by parents and peers. Scripture contains numerous exhortations that make this very point. Proverbs 22:6 encourages parents and others: "Train a child in the way he should go, and when he is old he will not turn from it." Proverbs 22:24–25 warns of our peers: "Do not make friends with a hot-tempered man, do not associate with one easily angered, or you may learn his ways and get yourself ensnared."

At the same time, Scripture does not absolve people of their crimes by shifting the blame to others. Instead the Bible places the blame squarely on the offender. A case in point is Nathan's confrontation of David over the latter's sin against Uriah and Bathsheba (2 Sam. 12:1–10).

The primary effect this model has on the Christian, however, is it focuses on society or environment and not on God in determining who the Christian is. The Bible teaches that God has initially designed each person in terms of his or her gifts, talents, and abilities. The mechanistic model divorces God from the process and places blame on or gives credit to parents, peers, and teachers. Consequently, Christians may look to the influence of others in the process rather than to God's unique design.

The Developmental Model

Proponents of the developmental model believe people can essentially become whoever or whatever they want to be in this life. It is possible for people to develop their skills, talents, and abilities and become the kind of people they admire and want to be. Thus the emphasis is on personal development and becoming something or someone else. One author writes, "Unlike behaviorists and psychoanalysts, who believe that your behavior is determined by your environment or your unconscious needs, humanists believe that you have control of your fate and are free to become whatever you are capable of being."[6]

Presently the New Age movement has picked up on this humanistic perspective and promoted it among its followers. They teach that because people are godlike, they have unlimited potential to be and do whatever they desire. This viewpoint was reflected by one American president who, when he accepted his party's nomination to run for the nation's highest office, said that a part of his dream for every child in this country was that someday they would be able to grow up to become whatever they wanted to be.

Numerous problems exist for this model. First, like the mechanistic model, it ignores God as part of the process. The focus is completely on man, without any reference to divine instruction. That is unacceptable for the Christian.

Second, few debate the idea that people can and should grow and develop their talents, skills, and abilities. The Savior experienced the same according to Luke 2:52. Yet this view fails to look at who a person is to begin with. The emphasis is on the future. Yet if man is basically good or even godlike, why does he have to become something other than who he already is?

Third, the view fails in the pragmatic realm. It does not work. Though some have been helped, things have not changed appreciably since this view became popular. In general, people continue to struggle with the same old problems of self-esteem and significance. People focus so much on who or what they want to become that they fail to discern and be satisfied with who they are. The latter is the key, not the former.

Finally and most important for believers, we cannot be or become whoever we want. As the rest of this chapter will show, God has designed all of us as unique, talented, and gifted individuals who do not need to become other than who we already are. Nothing is wrong with the way God has designed us. The issue is discovering and developing who you are, not becoming who you are not.

In spite of the many problems, it is common to hear the developmental model perpetuated in the Christian community. At Christian colleges, universities, and even seminaries, sincere students who desire to serve the Savior decide what they plan to do with their lives with little regard for who God has designed them to be. As described in the introduction, a young seminarian such as David plans to be a pastor without ever asking the question, *Has God designed me with the gifts, talents, and abilities necessary to function in the pastoral role?* As Mattson and Miller point out, the problem is that far too many clergy today "are not gifted at central requirements like preaching, teaching, and evangelism."[7] Others pursue a particular kind of pastoral ministry such as church planting or church revitalization without realizing that different situations call for different leadership styles and abilities. In addition, no two congregations are alike. Lyle Schaller concludes, "These differences among congregations also influence the style of ministerial leadership that is appropriate for a particular congregation at a certain stage of its life. These differences have also made obsolete the old cliché, 'Every minister should be able to serve any congregation.'"[8]

The Biblical Model

What does Scripture say about humankind and their design? Who are we? What role does God play in our developmental process? Both the Old and New Testaments provide a different picture of humankind from that portrayed by the deterministic and developmental models. The Bible articulates a design theology that places God's stamp on his creation. Both Testaments put God in the picture and teach that he has fashioned us with a wonderful, unique design. The biblical emphasis is not on the shaping role of the environment or our becoming something else. Instead the thrust of the Scriptures is on who you are as God's creative expression. So the question is not only, Who do you think you are? It's also, Who does God say you are?

The Old Testament

The Old Testament reflects a design theology. The concept of God as the master designer is displayed throughout his creation. In Psalm 19:1 David writes, "The heavens declare the glory of God; the skies proclaim the work of his hands." God is the sovereign Creator whose handiwork is evident not only in the beauty of the physical universe but in its design, from the function, precise placement, and circulation of the sun, moon, and planets (Gen. 1:14–19; Eccles. 1:5); to the circulation patterns of the winds and seas (Eccles. 1:6–7); right down to the intricate structure of a leaf.

The animal world reflects God's design. He created animal life on days five and six (Gen. 1:20–25). He divided the animal kingdom into various distinct species that reproduced "according to their kind." Each mirrors God's unique craftsmanship, as illustrated by the story "A Rabbit on the Swim Team."

Once upon a time, the animals decided they would do something meaningful to meet the problems of the new world. So they organized a school.

They adopted an activity curriculum of running, climbing, swimming, and flying. To make it easier to administer the curriculum, all the animals took all subjects.

The duck was excellent in swimming; in fact, he was better than his instructor. But he made only passing grades in flying and was very poor in running. Since he was slow in running, he had to drop swimming and stay after school to practice running. This caused his webbed feet to be so badly worn he became only average in swimming. But average was quite acceptable, so nobody worried about that—except the duck.

The rabbit started at the top of his class in running but developed a nervous twitch in his leg muscles because of so much makeup work in swimming.

The squirrel was excellent in climbing, but he encountered constant frustration in flying class because his teacher made him start from the ground up instead of from the treetop down. He developed a "charlie horse" from overexertion, and so only got a C in climbing and a D in running.

The eagle was a problem child and was severely disciplined for being a nonconformist. In climbing classes he beat all the others to the top of the tree but insisted on using his own way to get there.[9]

The lesson is obvious. God created each animal with a unique design to accomplish a distinct purpose. He designed ducks to swim, rabbits to run, squirrels to climb, and eagles to fly.

We, too, reflect God's special design. Genesis 1:27 records the creation of man, not in the image and likeness of the animal kingdom, but in the image and likeness of God. Thus we were created and designed to function as God's representatives on earth with dominion over the earth (Gen. 1:26–28; Ps. 8). God placed Adam in the garden "to work it and take care of it" (Gen. 2:15). There was for Adam a clear sense of meaning and purpose to his existence.

In several passages, the Old Testament presents God as the Potter and people as the clay vessels that he molds and shapes (Job 10:8–9; Ps. 119:73; Isa. 29:16; 64:8). The primary implication of this metaphor is that God is both Creator and sovereign Lord over man. The very figure itself hints of design. Molding and shaping implies designing. As a potter molds and shapes each vessel of clay, so God in the creative act designs humankind.

This design relates to both our immaterial and material aspects. In Psalm 139:13–16a, the psalmist writes, "For you created my inmost being; you knit me together in my mother's womb. I praise you because I am fearfully and wonderfully made; your works are wonderful, I know that full well. My frame was not hidden from you when I was made in the secret place. When I was woven together in the depths of the earth, your eyes saw my unformed body." In the passage, David is emphasizing God's sovereignty and superintendence over the creative processes relating to reproduction, even the immaterial or spiritual as well as the physical. Yet in the midst of this graphic but figurative language—the creating, knitting, weaving, and making, and the wonder of it all—the design aspect, though by no means the emphasis, is present.

God's creative design is also reflected in our skills, talents, and abilities. In the process of constructing the tabernacle, the Lord appointed certain craftsmen, in particular Bezalel and Oholiab, to engage in their areas of expertise—making artistic designs for gold, silver, and bronze; the cutting and setting of stones; and working with wood (Exod. 31:1–5). Verse 3 says that God filled Bezalel with the Spirit and gave special skill, ability, and knowledge to execute the project. The same is found in other texts: Exodus 28:3; 35:30–36:1. They were all skilled craftsmen by divine gift. Whether or not these skills were a part of their initial design from birth is not clear for the text does not indicate such. I suspect they were, and that is why they were selected to begin with. Regardless, God gave them the necessary skills and abilities or additional skills and abilities to accomplish the temple project.

Several other passages and some parallel passages in the Gospels and Epistles also suggest God's unique, personal design-stamp on people. In Jeremiah 1:4–5 the prophet writes, "The word of the Lord came to me, saying, 'Before I formed you in the womb I knew you, before you were born I set you apart; I appointed you as a prophet to the nations.'" Much the same is said of John the Baptist (Luke 1:13–17), the Messiah (Isa. 49:1–6), and

Paul (Gal. 1:15). The question is whether or not these are unique cases that would not be true of the rest of us. The biblical teaching on predestination, foreknowledge, and the divine will indicates that God does not sit up in heaven and capriciously guess at the future (Acts 2:23; 4:27–28). God knows all about us and our designs because he has determined them beforehand. However, he chose to reveal his design in a special way to Jeremiah, Zechariah, and Paul because of their unique circumstances.

The New Testament

The New Testament reflects a design theology as well. It is communicated through the concept of the body of Christ, the parable of the talents, and the biblical teaching on spiritual gifts. In 1 Corinthians 12:12–27 and Romans 12:4–5, Paul draws an analogy between believers who make up the church, the body of Christ, and the human body. As God's design is evident in the human body, so it is in the spiritual body—made up of all who are in Christ. Spiritual gifts in the church body reflect the principle of design (1 Cor. 12:1–11, 28–31).

What does this figure imply about our designs? First, God has sovereignly made us just the way we are—God is the Architect, the Master Designer, the Potter. Whether you are an ear or an eye, 1 Corinthians 12:18 teaches, "God has arranged the parts in the body, every one of them, just as he wanted them to be." Therefore, there is no need to be upset with our place or function in the body of Christ. Instead there is much satisfaction in knowing we are ministering in accordance with God's design and purpose for our lives. The key is discovering which body part you are, then functioning according to that design.

Second, God has made us different—a hand, an ear, or an eye (1 Cor. 12:14–17). While Christians may have similar designs, no two have the same design. When it comes to making people, God is not in the cookie cutting business—each of us is unique. Consequently Christians need to discover their different designs and places of service; they cannot do anything they want. As the story "A Rabbit on the Swim Team" illustrates, God designed ducks to swim and rabbits to run. When ducks attempt to run or rabbits try to swim, they are functioning outside their intended design, and serious problems soon develop. The same is true of people. An eye cannot serve God effectively as an ear, nor can an ear serve as an eye.

Third, while God has made us different, all of us are needed if the body is to function well (1 Cor. 12:14–17). A major problem for the church approaching the twenty-first century is "unemployment." Too many Christians have dropped out of church, joining the ranks of the unchurched across America. And those remaining tend to be involved as spectators. Larry Richards and his colleagues asked 5,000 pastors what the greatest needs are for strengthening the church. From a twenty-five-item list, nearly 100 percent gave a first or second priority to "Getting my lay people involved as ministering men and women."[10] I suspect that a major reason for this problem is the church's insistence on placing believers in ministry positions for which they are not designed—round pegs in square holes. In a short period of time, they burn out and drop out. Discovering our divine design is the key to implementing Ephesians 4:11–12 in the church.

Another passage in the New Testament that touches on God's divine design is the parable of the talents in Matthew 25:14–30. In this parable a master (God) decides to take a journey, leaving three servants in charge of his property. According to the ability of each one, he gives a certain amount of money ("talents") to invest. (Here the term *talents* is not to be confused with natural gifts or abilities.) One man doubles his five talents to ten and is well rewarded when the master returns (vv. 19–21). Another doubles his two and is also rewarded (vv. 22–23). However, the third accomplishes nothing with his single talent, and the master rebukes him and gives that talent to the first servant (vv. 24–28).

Several observations are important for the divine design concept. First, this parable is one of two parables following the disciples' request for Jesus to explain the destruction of the temple, the sign of his return, and the end of the age (Matt. 24:1–3). The two parables appear to address life as it will be at his return. The parable of the talents addresses how God's professed servants should use their God-given abilities for him until he returns.

Second, all the servants have differing abilities. Both the first and second are highly commended and rewarded, yet they are not the same. This holds true for Christians. All have various abilities worthy of the master's commendation and reward, yet some have more ability than others.

Third, the master understands the abilities of each servant and distributes the money accordingly. The one with the most ability is given the five talents and the one with the least is given only one talent. God also apparently distributes ministry opportunities on the basis of our abilities. God as Creator understands each person's design and does not ask us to accomplish more in life with those natural abilities than we are capable of. He did not give five talents to the servant who was only capable of handling one.

Fourth, the harsh treatment of the last servant involved his failure to discern who God is, which in turn led to his mishandling of the single talent. His failure was not that he was a one-talent person, for God rewarded the other two not according to their talents but their abilities. The point in verses 24 to 26 is that the man did not understand God's true character and failed to use his ability accordingly. God is not hard, harvesting where he does not sow and gathering where he has not cast seed. Based on his misunderstanding of the master's true character, the servant would not venture any risk and failed to invest his talent wisely. It is most important that Christians seek to use their God-given capabilities wisely, understanding God's true nature. Once we have discovered what those abilities are, we must understand God's provision and take risks to use those abilities to their fullest for Christ. Though God's judgment of us will not be as harsh as that of the wicked servant, who most likely was not a true believer (v. 30), service for the Savior is not to be viewed lightly.

A third portion of the New Testament that contributes to the divine design concept is the biblical teaching on spiritual gifts. Far too many in the body of Christ are not aware that this topic is in the Bible. Consequently they go through life never realizing that God has bestowed on them special abilities to make a vital contribution to his kingdom. When individual, gifted believers are not aware of their spiritual gifts and do not minister with them, the whole body of Christ is hindered in its effectiveness (1 Cor. 12:20–26). Some confuse spiritual gifts with other related areas of their design such as the ability to work with a particular age group. Others confuse them with the fruit of the Spirit in Galatians 5:22–23.

Scriptures that relate to God's spiritual gifts are found in 1 Corinthians 12, Romans 12, Ephesians 4, and 1 Peter 4. Spiritual gifts are God-given abilities to serve him in a particular manner in his kingdom. They are God-given for they come from him (1 Cor. 12:7; Eph. 4:7–11). He bestows them sovereignly so that each Christian has at least one as a part of his or her divine design (1 Cor. 12:11). They are distributed to each individually to make a distinctive contribution to the body as a whole (1 Cor. 12:7).

Worksheet

1. Do you have a strong desire to live a meaningful, fulfilling life while on this earth? Do you feel an inner compulsion to accomplish something of importance with your life? Why or why not?

2. Do you believe that up to this point you have made a significant contribution to your community, church, or family? Have you gained a deep sense of significance? Why or why not?

3. Do you know who you are—how God has designed you? Do you know why you are here, and what God wants to accomplish with your life? Have you realized your full potential for the kingdom of God? Why or why not?

4. Most likely you have been exposed directly or indirectly to the ideas that your environment has exclusively shaped you into who you are (deterministic model), or that you can be or do anything you want (developmental model). If so, which has most influenced you? When and where did this take place? Did this exposure come through your parents, teachers, peers, the media?

5. Has your exposure to these models influenced your thinking about your own abilities to serve God? If so, explain.

6. What are some of the passages or concepts in the Bible that teach the divine design? As you read this chapter, did any other passages come to mind? If so, what are they?

7. Can you think of any arguments or reasons other than those in the Bible that imply or illustrate the divine design concept?

The Importance of
Your Divine Design

2

What Difference Does It Make?

There was little question in Carol's mind that God wanted her to be an attorney. She got her start in the field as a part-time clerk during her first year at law school in south Texas. And she was good at it. It did not take the firm long to realize her potential, so by the time of her graduation she was practically functioning as an attorney with two clerks and one secretary—even though she had not taken the bar exam. She loved every minute of it—the challenge, the intrigue, and the people. When her husband had a job transfer, she easily relocated and quickly adapted to a similar position in a branch firm in their new city.

Though she had completely devoted her life to Christ, Carol believed her full-time ministry was to be a good attorney. Still, she craved meaningful involvement in her church for many reasons. Its ministry had become important to both her and her husband. Many exciting things were happening, convincing her that God had wonderful plans for this rapidly growing congregation. Carol was thrilled when several of her friends at work visited the church and in time embraced the Savior. She and her husband could not have children, so they decided to invest a significant portion of their lives in ministry in the church. They had become serious Christians intent on accomplishing authentic ministry for their Savior. They did not have a lot of discretionary time, however, so what was available needed to be invested wisely.

One item of immense importance in Carol's life was her divine design, her ministry identity. Her understanding of this would determine what Christ would accomplish through her life and ministry both at work and in the church.

The divine design concept is important in two ways for Carol, her husband, and all who are serious about serving Christ whether on a part-time basis in a church or in a vocational Christian ministry. The first is personal and the other is institutional.

The importance of the divine design concept for each Christian is practically unlimited. Three areas, however, stand out.

Knowing Who You Are

First, it is important that you know who you are. Initially this could pose a threat. You may fear probing your design because in the past you have taken psychological tests designed to uncover pathological problems (sin problems). While this can prove spiritually valuable, it can also be a frightening and disconcerting experience. There is an analytical side to assessment, often associated with the field of psychological counseling, that uses tools such as the Minnesota Multiphasic Personality Inventory (MMPI) to discover emotional abnormality or dysfunctional behavior (these are problems in the area of your "flesh" or "sinful nature" described in Galatians 5:16–21). Whether you use these tools or not, it is critical to any ministry for Christ that you understand where your sin problems lie and that you deal with them.

On the other hand, not only should we discover what is wrong with us, we can and must discover what is right with us. The former explores our depravity, which is beyond the scope of this book, while the latter explores our dignity, which is the purpose of this book.[1] And it is the latter that represents the positive side of knowing our identity—who we really are.[2] The following will put this into perspective.

Divine Design

Discovering who you are involves discerning your divine design. The process delves into two critical areas—your capabilities and limitations.

Capabilities

Your capabilities are your spiritual gifts, passion, temperament, natural talents and gifts, and other abilities that you have from God. They reside with each of us who knows Christ as personal Savior, and in a sense are waiting to be discovered so they can be used in service for Christ. In fact, it would seem strange that believers would not be excited and vitally interested in discovering the abilities with which God has blessed them. Everybody is a 10 somewhere,[3] and the discovery of your design helps to determine precisely where.

While you can grow and develop in many areas, your capabilities are sovereignly assigned by God and will not change over time. They do not change in essence before or after conversion. Consultants Mattson and Miller write:

> Our evidence demonstrates that motivational patterns do not change when a person becomes a Christian. The ingredients seen prior to conversion are seen after conversion. This is disturbing to people who expect it to be otherwise, but perhaps we will better understand our position in Christ if we see that God's intention for us is not replacement of who we are, but redemption of who we are. God's creation of us, including our basic motivational pattern, is not bad. . . . Conversion has us rejoicing in the fact that we are enabled to become who we originally were made to be, rather than becoming someone entirely different. The renewal takes place when we are resurrected in conversion; and sanctification causes a radical change, not in the gift we have, but in its purpose and use.[4]

Therefore it would be a waste of time to ask God to give us different spiritual gifts or to change us to another temperament.

Limitations

Our limitations are the gifts, passion, and natural abilities we do not have as a part of our makeup.[5] God in his sovereignty has decided not to give us certain tools as a part of our design. Consequently we must not view their absence as weakness nor ourselves as weak in these areas, but limited when we attempt to accomplish some aspect of ministry that calls for their use.

This does not mean we should avoid them entirely because that is not practical. Anyone who has been in ministry knows that is not realistic. It does mean we will not function as well when we find ourselves attempting to minister with them. This also means we will not derive as much satisfaction from their use. For example, you may not have the gift of teaching. There will be times, however, when out of necessity you may have to teach. You will not do it as effectively or enjoy it as much as someone with the gift, but you do it anyway.

From the standpoint of ministry preparation, it would not be wise to focus a significant amount of time on developing those areas that are not a part of your ministry design. The principle is to maximize your time in the area of your capabilities, not in the area of your limitations. You may experience some improvement, but it will not be significant enough to warrant the time spent. When I was in seminary, students were required to declare a major in a particular department. Some students chose to major in a department that focused on their limitations with the hope that somehow they might see significant improvement. In retrospect, this was a mistake. They would have been better prepared for ministry had they focused on a department that enhanced their capabilities, not their limitations.

Knowing our limitations can work to our ministry advantage in two ways. One is avoiding ministry burnout. Involving yourself in a ministry that calls for a divine design that is different from your own will, over a short period of time, lead to ministry burnout and, in time, ministry dropout. Instead you should invest a bare minimum of 60 percent of your time in a ministry area that matches your divine design. Anything less increases the chances for burnout proportionately.

The other advantage is that knowing our limitations aids us in working toward maximum ministry effectiveness. By knowing what we do not do well, we can focus significant time on what we do well. An important by-product of the process is we learn when to say no. For example, if someone approached you about teaching a class of adolescents or about teaching on a seminary level, you could say no based on the fact that you are not gifted in the area of teaching. It does not mean you might not substitute teach for a week. It does mean you will pursue areas of ministry more appropriate to your design.

Personal Character

Discovering who you are involves discerning your character. This also involves two areas—your character strengths and weaknesses.

Character Strengths

Your character is the foundation of your ministry whether you minister from the perspective of a lay person or someone involved in vocational Christian ministry. It is the essential element that qualifies you to minister to others. Unlike your divine design, God does not sovereignly predetermine your character. Rather, it is subject to change and must be developed. In fact, the development of Christian character is a lifetime process.

Character involves *being* and is a matter of your heart; whereas, your design involves *doing* and is a matter of your gifts, talents, and abilities. For you to be effective in ministry over the long haul, being must precede doing, because what you do (your ministry) flows out of who you are (your character). If doing should ever exceed being, then the development and exercise of your design will ultimately suck the life out of your heart, and you will crash and burn.

Our character strengths are those positive traits that conform to Christ's character—our Christlikeness. Scripture refers to numerous character qualities that enhance the life of the believer. Representative is Paul's list of specific character qualities in 1 Thessalonians 2:2–8 that enhanced his ministry. One quality described in verse 2 is *courage*. Ministry has its ups and downs. In the down times, it takes men and women of courage who are willing to take faith-risks to serve the Savior. Hebrews 11 spotlights several faith cameos of courageous people who trusted God during ministry down times.

Another quality in verse 2 is *endurance*. Those who serve Christ in any way must not be too quick to quit. Most often it is through endurance of difficult situations that we learn our greatest spiritual lessons. A quick study of those who have achieved significant ministries reveals that they have the ability to hang tough rather than quit and run.

In verse 3 Paul reveals the character qualities of *integrity, purity,* and *honesty.* If we have any problems in these areas, the entire ministry suffers the consequences. Christian ministry in the 1980s and early 1990s has suffered adversely at the hands of professionals who professed Christ publicly but lacked personal integrity, purity of motive, and individual honesty.

Finally in verse 7 Paul describes his *gentleness* and *affection,* comparing himself to a caring mother. In verse 8 he assures those under his ministry of his affection. It is amazing what others can accomplish when they know we love them.

Scripture also cites specific character qualities as essential for leaders and followers. In 1 Timothy 3:1–13 and Titus 1:5–9 we find essential qualities for elders and deacons, such as self-control, respect, discipline, hospitality, gentleness, honesty, and trustworthiness. We find additional character qualities for leaders in Acts 6:3–5, such as the filling of the Spirit, faith, and wisdom. Scripture encourages every Christian to work toward maturity and Christlikeness (Gal. 4:19; 1 Cor. 11:1; Eph. 4:13), to live by the Spirit (Gal. 5:16), and to evidence the fruit of the Spirit: love, joy, peace, patience, kindness, goodness, faithfulness, gentleness, and self-control (Gal. 5:22–23).

Character Weaknesses

Discovering who you are will uncover weaknesses in character as well as strengths. While the term *limitations* refers to certain gifts, temperaments, and abilities that are outside your divine design, the term *weaknesses* best refers to the negative character traits present to some extent in all believers regardless of their design. These traits will always be with us because no one will achieve perfection while in this present body (Phil. 3:10–14). That is why a large portion of Scripture addresses spiritual growth and maturity.

Our character weaknesses must be discovered and dealt with. These "emotional splinters" constantly work their way to the surface and cause us much pain in our relationships with others and with God. While we cannot change our designs, we can alter our negative character qualities and should attempt to deal with them regularly with God's help. This is the intent of Romans 6–8. Psychological testing and counsel can help us identify some of the "splinters" and force them to the surface, where we can properly handle them with Scripture.

Life's Circumstances

Discovering who you are involves discerning your life's circumstances. This process examines such areas as your age, marital status, race, education, gender, and health.

Age

We are never too young or old to have a ministry in the body of Christ. Ministering on a part-time basis is possible for any Christian regardless of age. The divine design of a child is discernable at an early age. Parents would be wise to observe their children's ministry makeup and begin to encourage them to pursue certain ministries in the church even at an early age.

Ministry in a full-time situation, however, does have some age restrictions. Particularly in the church environment the current trend is to recruit pastors between their twenties and fifties, with the exception of those who minister to senior citizens. In the 1990s the average age of those entering seminaries climbed to nearly thirty, and an increasing number of Christians are pursuing vocational ministry as a second career. In the past, the practice was for pastors to stay in the pulpit until God took them home. Today churches are discouraging this practice and tend not to hire men as senior pastors who are in their fifties or older.

Marital Status

For most ministry positions, married people are preferred over singles and the nondivorced over divorced Christians, especially in vocational (full-time, compensated) ministry. In the past this was because there were more marrieds than singles and more nondivorced than divorced, but the figures are shifting.

Divorced Christians carry a certain stigma with them regardless of the situation. The Baby Boom and Bust generations, however, seem more accepting of pastors who have experienced a divorce. While theologians debate the impact of divorce on the qualifications of those who pursue vocational Christian ministry in general and pastoral ministry in particular, most agree that it does not negate one's divine design. Regardless, it is much easier for divorced Christians to minister nonvocationally than vocationally.

Race

A Christian's race should not affect his or her service for Christ.
While Scripture acknowledges the difference between races (for example, Jews and Gentiles), it does not place any one race above another
(Gal. 3:28). In fact, Scripture does not tolerate discrimination on racial grounds, and the early church took action in such situations (Acts
6:1–7).

The issue of race becomes important in vocational ministry when we
consider the homogeneous principle developed by missiologist Donald
A. McGavran. The principle states that "Men like to become Christians
without crossing racial, linguistic, or class barriers."[6] In effect it teaches
that ministry is most effective among those who are of the same race,
language, or social class as the minister, especially in evangelizing lost
people. This has become one of the most controversial principles in the
Church Growth movement, and its critics attack it as racist and classist.

To be fair to McGavran, however, I must say that he is not arguing
that this is the way things ought to be or that ministries should discriminate on the basis of race, language, or class. He is arguing that in most
situations people of the same race, language, or class tend to minister
best to one another, whether to Christians or non-Christians.

There are various reasons for this. One is that people from the same
group understand best the culture, needs, and aspirations of those most
like them. Another is that lost people generally think and act with an
awareness of race and culture. Most will be attracted to a church where
the people are like them in some way. I refer to this as the affinity factor.
A third is that no church can be culturally neutral, and most people are
attracted to a church that is closest to their culture. Regardless, it is a
biblical imperative that a church must never discriminate for any reason against anyone on the basis of race, language, or class.[7]

Education

Our educational level impacts our ministry. Whether right or wrong,
someone of inferior education will have difficulty ministering to those
with an exceptional education. An education or the lack thereof affects
the individual's ministry credibility. In a day when professionalism is at a
premium, those who are considered unprofessional are at a distinct dis-

advantage. In most situations, people prefer that ministers have an education that is equivalent to or beyond their own. This is true in terms of nonvocational ministry and especially true of those in vocational ministry. It is difficult to pursue vocational ministry or training for ministry without certain basic educational credentials—a high school or college diploma.

Gender

In the past, women have been in the majority of those actively serving the Savior in nonvocational ministry. Those who have grown up in the church can usually remember a woman who had an impact in their lives for the Savior—but not a man, besides a pastor. Professional ministry and higher leadership positions, however, have been dominated by men.

In the second half of the twentieth century this has begun to change. More women are finding professional positions on ministry teams. Some churches have women on their leadership boards serving as elders and deacons. The evangelical wing of the church has debated what the Bible teaches regarding women's role in ministry in general and the church in particular. Can women be pastors of churches or elders on church boards? Can they teach men? Each Christian and each ministry must study this issue and follow through in ministry accordingly.

Health

For obvious reasons, those in good physical health have an advantage over those in poor health. Regardless of a person's divine design or spiritual character, poor health or disabilities can limit ministry in several ways. One is a person's ability to minister at all. Someone confined to a wheelchair might have difficulty functioning as a traveling evangelist. Some Christians find it healthier to live in some areas than in others. Allergies can limit some ministries to a state such as Arizona.

Not only can one's own health affect a ministry, the poor health of a spouse or child can have the same limiting effect. The important thing to remember in any of these situations is that God is sovereign in our affairs (Dan. 4:17, 25, 32). We should attempt to serve him as best we can in the context of any particular health limitations.

Liking Who You Are

A second personal benefit of *knowing* who you are is *liking* who you are. The offices of Christian counselors and pastors are inundated with people who are struggling with poor self-esteem. The growing number of emotional and spiritual self-help books and articles indicates that the problem is becoming epidemic in proportion. Far too many Christians look in the mirror and dislike what they see. In many cases they habitually evaluate themselves in terms of their depravity and not their dignity. They have little knowledge of themselves and dislike what knowledge they do have. The result is a profound sense of insignificance and low self-worth.

The Command

Scripture teaches in a positive way that we should love ourselves. Jesus commands, "Love your neighbor as yourself" (Matt. 19:19). Paul conveys the same principle when he tells husbands "to love their wives as their own bodies. He who loves his wife loves himself. After all, no one ever hated his own body, but he feeds and cares for it, just as Christ does the church" (Eph. 5:28–29). And again in verse 33 he writes, "However, each one of you also must love his wife as he loves himself, and the wife must respect her husband."

The Problem

When Paul and Jesus command Christians to love others as they love themselves, are they advocating some form of narcissism? This would clearly cut against the grain of biblical truth. So much of Scripture addresses our responsibility to put others before ourselves. In Philippians 2:3–4, Paul exhorts believers, "Do nothing out of selfish ambition or vain conceit, but in humility consider others better than yourselves. Each of you should look not only to your own interests, but also to the interests of others." And in verse 21, he speaks negatively of those who put their own interests first: "For everyone looks out for his own interests, not those of Jesus Christ." Again in 1 Corinthians 10:24, Paul writes, "Nobody should seek his own good, but the good of others." Finally, one of the qualities of love mentioned in the great love chapter of the Bible, 1 Corinthians 13, is that "it is not self-seeking" (v. 5).

The Solution

The solution to this apparent contradiction lies as usual in a careful handling of the texts in their context. The key passages to unraveling the mystery are Ephesians 5:29 and 5:33. Paul follows his exhortation to love oneself in verse 28 with verse 29, which clarifies the meaning of the abstract concept of love with a concrete example—caring for and feeding the physical body. Certainly the physical acts of caring for and feeding one's physical body are self-focused. Yet most agree that they are necessary and vital to other acts that are others-focused and therefore are not to be considered narcissistic.

Verse 33 sheds more light on the meaning of the "love oneself" concept and introduces the emotional element. After Paul tells the husband to "love his wife as he loves himself," he again follows with a concrete statement that helps define what he means by the abstract term *love*. He adds, "and the wife must respect her husband." The key term here is *respect*. It is Paul's clarification of what he means by self-love—it involves self-respect. Consequently, loving yourself involves taking care of yourself physically and emotionally. These are necessary, permissible requirements if you are to function well in ministry.

The Implication

A critical factor in loving ourselves biblically is liking ourselves. That is where discerning our divine design is so important. It reveals our gifts, talents, and abilities in a favorable light. We discover what is good about ourselves as well as what is not so good. We maintain a healthy balance in the awareness of both our depravity and our dignity. Then, once our design is deployed in the proper ministry environment, we have an added, powerful sense of significance and incentive for more ministry that delights our souls and honors the Savior.

Being Who You Are

A third personal benefit of knowing your divine design is that *knowing* and *liking* who you are naturally leads to *being* who you are. The former creates a powerful thirst for the latter, and the result is authenticity.

The Problem

People who do not like who they are often attempt to avoid who they are or try to be someone else. They put on false masks and play roles so others will not discover their identity and unmask their perceived ugliness. They fear that if people find out who they are, they will not like them and will reject them. If they do not like themselves, then it is only logical that others will not like them either. The pain from this would prove unbearable and must be avoided at all costs. The thing farthest from their minds is living authentically or modeling vulnerability.

The Solution

The solution is discerning our divine design. When we discover who we are in Christ and how God has uniquely designed each of us after his image to contribute in a significant, meaningful way to his kingdom, we are free to be authentic. But what is authenticity? It is integrity from core to crust.[8] What you see is what you get—personal reality. We take off our masks and stop playing fictitious roles because we know and like who we really are and no longer are ashamed of what God has made. The result? An authentic life that produces authentic ministry.

Another by-product is vulnerability. Those who do not know or like who they are, whether Christian or non-Christian, are not vulnerable people. Vulnerability means sharing Christ's strength in the context of our weakness.[9] William Lawrence writes, "It is the appropriate disclosure of an older brother or sister's pilgrimage that focuses on Christ in His conviction, faithfulness, grace, and blessing in such a way that attention turns to Him and the developing leader is encouraged, released from sin, and motivated to grow in confidence and impact."[10] Only as we become convinced of the wonder and beauty of our design and accept ourselves as God accepts us can we truly be vulnerable.

Over time our self-image blooms and matures as we discover a new freedom in Christ that we may never have realized in the past. In John 8:31–32 Christ says, "If you hold to my teaching, you are really my disciples. Then you will know the truth, and the truth will set you free." Truth has a liberating effect. And the truth of knowing, liking, and being who Christ has designed us to be frees us to become his special kingdom people.

The Organizational Importance of Your Design

How might the divine design concept help ministry organizations in general and churches in particular? When the leaders and the people in a church or other Christian organization discover their divine designs, the ministry benefits as a whole. Before going through the discovery process, many organizations are like an eight-cylinder car hitting on three or four cylinders. However, after completing the discovery process, they drive away a well-tuned machine hitting without a miss on all eight cylinders.

The Principle

New Testament ministry is team ministry. The concept is sprinkled throughout its pages. First, Christ ministered in a team context. He is God; thus he could have accomplished his ministry with a simple command. He chose instead to minister and pursue the Father's will through a small band of faltering Palestinian disciples. He began by traveling and teaching from village to village, calling the Twelve to himself. This led to his sending them out in pairs (Mark 6:7). Later, according to Luke 10:1, he appointed seventy-two others who were also sent out in pairs.

Second, Paul ministered through a team. Rather than attempt to fulfill the Great Commission mandate alone, he opted for a team. The initial team consisted of Barnabas and Paul (Acts 11:22–30). On the first church-planting journey, Paul added Mark to the team (Acts 13:2–3, 5). On the second, Silas (Acts 15:40), Timothy (Acts 16:1–3), Luke (Acts 16), and others (Acts 18) joined the three. Finally, additional people were added or used to form new teams (Acts 19–20).

The Problem

Reality teaches that people, even completely committed Christians, may experience difficulties and heartache in attempting to work together. This was true for the Savior, who was constantly disappointed by the disciples; he was denied by Peter and betrayed by Judas. Before commencing the second missionary journey, Paul and Barnabas had a significant disagreement over whether or not to bring John Mark back on the team, because he had deserted them earlier. According to Acts 15:37–40, they agreed to disagree and pursue separate ministries. Interestingly, while Paul and Barnabas chose not to work together, they did not abandon the team concept (Acts 15:39–40). If godly men like Paul and Barnabas struggled as a team, then serious lay people and ministry professionals are sure to struggle as well.

In addition to personal problems between team members, there is the problem of placing the wrong person in the wrong position on the team. Every ministry team will experience differences of opinion; some churches further exacerbate the problem by misplacing team members. We have all experienced the ecstasy of working on a good team and the agony of working on a bad one. As in athletics, it is critical that the right player be put in the right position to make a good ministry team. As long as the quarterback plays his position, the team has a chance to win. If the coach decides to move his quarterback to offensive tackle, the results can be disastrous.

The fact that so many ministry teams are voluntary organizations does not help matters. Lay people working on a team in a church context have the option to quit and move to another ministry at the slightest provocation. Staff people do not have the same freedom. They have more to lose, and therefore the chances are better that they will work out a resolution to their problems.

The Solution

A solution is the discovery of our design. Scripture makes an analogy between the human body and the church (Rom. 12 and 1 Cor. 12). Just as the body has various parts, such as a hand, an eye, arms, and legs, which are necessary for the body to function well in life, so the church is made up of different body parts that are crucial to the functioning of the body in ministry (1 Cor. 12:27).

The purpose of a quality program of assessment is to help Christian hands discover that they are hands and to begin to function as hands and not as feet or toes.[11] The ministry organization or church determines what it wants to accomplish. Then it recruits the appropriate lay and vocational people who best fit by design the various positions on the ministry team. The result is fewer problems among team members and more efficiency in ministry. If a ministry wants to reach out to street people in an urban area, it must look for someone with a passion for "down and outers" and the gifts of leadership and mercy. If an organization decides to plant a church, it looks for a church planter. If a plateaued or dying church wants to change its course and cast a new vision for ministry, it must find a change agent with a passion for reviving established churches.

Worksheet

1. Have you taken psychological tests that can surface emotional problems (such as the Minnesota Multiphasic Personality Inventory)? Does taking these inventories frighten you? How is discovering your divine design different?

2. What is the difference between capabilities and limitations in your divine design? Can you change your capabilities or limitations? Explain. Would it be wise to spend a lot of time attempting to develop in the area of your limitations? Does this mean that you totally ignore your limitations? Explain.

3. What is the difference between strengths and weaknesses in your personal character? Why are the terms *strengths* and *weaknesses* used of your character but not your divine design? Would it be wise to spend a lot of time improving your weaknesses? Explain.

4. How would your age, marital status, race, education, sex, or health be a factor in your ministry?

5. At this point in your life, do you like who you are? Why or why not? What effect do the exhortations to love yourself in Matthew 19:19 and Ephesians 5:28–29, 33 have on your liking who you are? Explain.

6. Do you find yourself wearing masks and playing roles to hide what you believe is your real identity? Why? What impact does this have on your ability to be authentic and minister authentically? How has it affected your vulnerability?

7. Are you currently ministering in a team context? Why or why not? If you are ministering on a ministry team, how well is the team functioning together? How would you explain this situation? Would discovering each member's unique, divine design help the team function better?

The Components of 3
Your Divine Design

What Are the Pieces of Your Puzzle?

Tom was sleeping like a baby. It felt so good to wake up in the morning feeling rested and refreshed. No barking dog or passing car could shake him out of his slumber. What had changed his nights so dramatically and chased away his insomnia? The simple but monumental answer is not only had he graduated from college, but he also had made a decision regarding life after college. His decision was to pursue vocational Christian ministry, and he was profoundly excited about it. Another answer concerning his life's purpose had fallen in place for him.

What were the circumstances that affected Tom's decision for full-time ministry? The Bible study he attended in a campus dorm had begun a study of spiritual gifts. Before that, he had no idea that God had given him certain abilities for service to others.

But Tom has uncovered only a part of all that God has done for him in his divine design for ministry. This design is like a puzzle made up of a number of pieces. At this point only one piece of the puzzle—spiritual gifts—is in place. What are the other pieces? Some of the components that provide him and all Christians with the big picture of God's design are spiritual gifts, passion, temperament, leadership role and style, evangelism style, and natural gifts and talents. Read this chapter carefully and prayerfully because you will use its contents as a vehicle in the next chapter to discover your divine design.

Spiritual Gifts

Discerning your personal design for ministry involves discovering your spiritual gifts. They are an important component or piece of the puzzle of your life. But what are spiritual gifts? To whom are they given? What are the individual gifts?

The Definition of Spiritual Gifts

A spiritual gift is a unique, God-given ability for service.[1]

First, a spiritual gift is unique. Not every believer has the same spiritual gift. In 1 Corinthians 12, Paul draws an analogy between the human body and the body of Christ—the church. In 1 Corinthians 12:14 he focuses on the body: "Now the body is not made up of one part but of many." In verses 15–17 he points to the uniqueness of the various parts of the body by singling out the foot, hand, ear, and eye. In verse 27 he applies this "body truth" to the church: "Now you are the body of Christ, and each one of you is a part of it." In verses 29–31 he closes the chapter with a series of questions that point to the uniqueness of each person's gifts: "Are all apostles? Are all prophets? Are all teachers? Do all work miracles? Do all have gifts of healing? Do all speak in tongues? Do all interpret?" It is obvious in the English and definite in the original language that the expected answer to each question is no.[2]

The greatest value of spiritual gifts is that they are unique and complementary. The human body functions poorly as only an eye or an ear (1 Cor. 12:17). All the body parts are necessary to function fully with maximum effectiveness. In the same way, the church of Jesus Christ functions best when different gifts come together to complement one another in ministry for Christ.

Second, in addition to being unique, a spiritual gift is God-given. According to Scripture, all three members of the Godhead are involved in the distribution of our spiritual gifts. First, God the Father has a part in assigning our gifts. In Romans 12:3 Paul warns Christians against false pride. He encourages us instead to think about ourselves soberly. Then he adds, "in accordance with the measure of faith God has given you." Second, Jesus Christ, the Son, has assigned gifts to us. Paul writes in Ephesians 4:7–11: "But to each one of us grace has been given as Christ apportioned it. . . . He . . . gave gifts to men. . . . It was he who gave some to be apostles, some to be prophets, some to be evangelists, and some to be pastors and teachers." Third, the Holy Spirit distributes gifts. In a reference to spiritual gifts, Paul writes in 1 Corinthians 12:11: "All these are the work of one and the same Spirit, and he gives them to each one, just as he determines."

The reason for the involvement of all three members of the Godhead in disbursing gifts to the body is not stated in Scripture. However, other situations with this kind of divine involvement have been profound, momentous occasions, as in the work of creation and the cross. This underlines the importance of the biblical concept of spiritual gifts and encourages their discovery.

Third, spiritual gifts are certain abilities or capacities that are unique and God-given. Christians have spiritual gifts that grant them the abilities to accomplish various ministry functions. In this sense they have much in common with natural gifts or talents. A believer may have the natural ability to sing well, to play a musical instrument, to write novels or poetry, or to paint portraits. In a similar manner God gives Christians unusual abilities in such areas as teaching, leading, helping, shepherding, and evangelizing. The difference is the former are in some way present at birth and associated with natural birth; whereas the latter are given at the time of conversion and are associated only with the new birth.

As a person grows toward adulthood in life, it can be exciting, whether Christian or non-Christian, to discover the natural talents and abilities God has given. One individual may discover unusual abilities in basketball or tennis. How much excitement and fulfillment there must be in shooting a basketball well and experiencing all the right moves on the court. The same excitement and fulfillment can be present when believers discover and experience their spiritual gifts. Why would any serious Christian not want to know and exercise these special divine enablements?

Finally, spiritual gifts are unique, God-given abilities for service. Though Scripture recognizes that not all Christians will become involved in full-time service for Christ, it does not condone noninvolvement. Any person who professes Christ should be involved in the service of Christ. God has not given us special, spiritual abilities to enable us to sit on the sidelines—he wants us in the game (1 Peter 4:10).

Since these gifts are spiritual gifts, they are used for spiritual service. For example, the gift of teaching involves teaching Scripture and not just any topic. Only Christians have the God-given ability to teach the Bible with spiritual power and insight. The ability to teach other subject areas, such as mathematics, English, and history, are natural gifts, not spiritual gifts. God has given these natural abilities to unbelievers as well as believers for the good of humankind (common grace).

The Direction of Spiritual Gifts

Spiritual gifts are directed to believers, not unbelievers. In four passages of Scripture, three penned by Paul and one by Peter, it is clear that God has given his gifts to every believer. Note the use of "each one" in the following verses (the italics are mine).

But to *each one* of us grace has been given as Christ apportioned it (Eph. 4:7).

Now to *each one* the manifestation of the Spirit is given for the common good (1 Cor. 12:7).

All these are the work of one and the same Spirit, and he gives them to *each one*, just as he determines (1 Cor. 12:11).

Each one should use whatever gift he has received to serve others, faithfully administering God's grace in its various forms (1 Peter 4:10).

The fact that God gives every believer a gift implies that each has at least one gift. The biblical evidence indicates, however, that some, if not most, have multiple gifts. Paul identifies at least three gifts of his own in 1 Timothy 2:7 and 2 Timothy 1:11: a herald (preacher), an apostle, and a teacher. It is possible that he had the gifts of evangelism and leadership, for his passion was to preach the gospel to the Gentiles (Acts 22:21; 26:17), and he appears to have been the leader of various ministry teams (Acts 13:7; 15:40; 16:3).

A helpful concept in determining multigiftedness is the believer's gift-mix and gift-clusters.[3] Your *gift-mix* is a term that describes all your spiritual gifts. Your *gift-cluster* focuses on a clearly dominant gift that is supported by the other gifts in the cluster. For example, your gift-mix might consist of the gifts of leadership, administration, evangelism, teaching, and helps (figure 1). Your gift-cluster will contain a single, dominant gift—in this case evangelism—which is supported by the other four gifts (figure 2).

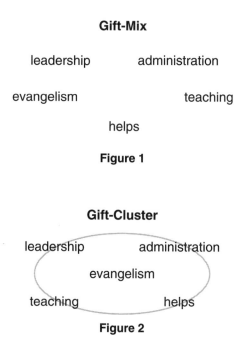

Gift-Mix

leadership   administration

evangelism   teaching

helps

Figure 1

Gift-Cluster

leadership   administration

evangelism

teaching   helps

Figure 2

Although many believers are multigifted, no believer has all the gifts. Again, the body metaphor in 1 Corinthians 12 makes this clear. The body of Christ is made up of a multiplicity of parts because no single part is sufficient of itself. The point is that we desperately need one another (1 Cor. 12:21–22). Carol's small church in south Texas is biblically inaccurate when it expects the pastor to do all the work of the ministry ("After all, that's what we pay him for"). The fact that every believer is gifted argues that every believer is needed. When people hold back from ministry, they affect the entire body of believers as well as themselves.

The Description of Spiritual Gifts

The fact that the Godhead has sovereignly bestowed on each Christian one or more spiritual gifts raises several questions: What are the gifts? How would you know one if you saw it, either in yourself or in another person? Before answering these questions, I need to briefly address two issues.

The first concerns the number of gifts. Are all the gifts available to Christians mentioned in the Bible? Do other spiritual gifts exist that are not found in Scripture? The Bible seems to indicate there might be other gifts. In both 1 Timothy 2:7 and 2 Timothy 1:11 Paul mentions preaching ("herald") along with the gifts of apostle and teaching. Although preaching (herald) is not listed among the gifts in Romans 12, 1 Corinthians 12, or Ephesians 4, in practice, it is apparent that some have a special ability to communicate Scripture better than others.[4]

Most likely many other gifts exist. However, we must be careful when we attempt to speak where Scripture does not. We can speak with certainty and authority regarding the gifts present in the Bible but with less certainty and authority regarding those that are not.

The second issue is, Are all the gifts mentioned in the Bible still operative and available to Christians today? The focus of this question is the sign gifts of healings, miracles, tongues, and the interpretation of tongues. Godly, evangelical scholars land on both sides of this issue, which would seem to indicate that Scripture is not entirely clear.[5] I have chosen not to discuss these and certain other gifts because of the divisive debate that surrounds them and because we are not sure what they were or how they were used in ministry. A more positive approach is to examine the gifts that most people agree are available today.

Unfortunately the Bible does not offer a precise definition of each spiritual gift. Perhaps Paul and others felt no need to attempt this because their use was so common in the first century. I base the following descriptions on what Scripture does say about the gifts and on my personal ministry experience with Christians.

Administration (1 Cor. 12:28)

The gift of administration is the God-given ability to manage or order the affairs of a church or parachurch organization. It could involve several

areas. One is working with leaders to determine ministry goals and then design a plan and budget to accomplish them. Another is creating an organizational structure around the plan and staffing that ministry structure.
Third is monitoring the plan and solving problems as they arise. Often the
mark of an administrator is the ability to accomplish this in a "fitting and
orderly way" (1 Cor. 14:40). This gift is not to be confused with that of leadership (Rom. 12:8), as the two are distinguished in the Bible.

Scripture presents examples of people with administrative gifts. Those
who stand out for their administrative abilities in the Old Testament are Joseph and Jethro. Paul's directions to Titus might indicate that he had the
spiritual gift of administration: "The reason I left you in Crete was that you
might straighten out what was left unfinished and appoint elders in every
town, as I directed you" (Titus 1:5). The gift of administration would have
proved helpful during certain church meetings at Corinth (1 Cor. 14:40).

Apostleship (1 Cor. 12:28; Eph. 4:11)

The gift of apostleship is included here but not as the primary gift exercised by the twelve apostles. They are the men whom God used, along
with New Testament prophets, to lay the foundation of the church (Eph.
2:20) and whose authoritative ministries were authenticated by certain
sign gifts (2 Cor. 12:12). They literally witnessed the resurrection of Christ
(Acts 1:8).

The gift of apostleship is used here in a secondary sense of people such
as Barnabas (Acts 14:4, 14), Silvanus and Timothy (1 Thess. 1:1; 2:6), and
Andronicus and Junias (Rom. 16:7). These were gifted individuals who
were apparently sent out by the churches for ministry that often involved
church planting. This gift may have included the capacity to minister cross-
culturally (Eph. 3:7–8).

Evangelism (Eph. 4:11)

The gift of evangelism is the ability to communicate clearly the gospel of
Jesus Christ (1 Cor. 15:1–4) to unbelievers individually or in a group context with the result that people respond and accept Christ. Believers with
this gift care passionately about lost people and have a strong desire to see
them come to faith. They feel compassion for them and authentically address their questions and their doubts. Thus lost people respond to their

presence positively. People with the gift of evangelism become frustrated when they go for a long period of time without sharing their faith and gain great satisfaction in equipping others to share their faith.

In the New Testament, Philip had the gift of evangelism and was referred to as "Philip the evangelist" (Acts 21:8). He is seen in Acts 8 witnessing individually to the Ethiopian eunuch. Timothy may have had the gift. In 2 Timothy 4:5 Paul encouraged him to do "the work of an evangelist." According to Ephesians 4:11–12, a primary function of those with the gift of evangelism is to equip others in the body of Christ for evangelism.

Encouragement (Rom. 12:8)

The gift of encouragement (or exhortation) involves encouraging, consoling, and when necessary confronting and admonishing others so they are benefited spiritually in their walk with Christ. Christians with this gift have unusual sensitivity for and are attracted to those who are discouraged or struggling. People tend to pursue them for counsel. As a result of their ministry, believers are drawn closer to Christ or are won back to Christ. An excellent example is Barnabas. His name means Son of Encouragement (Acts 4:36). He encouraged such men as Paul (Acts 9:27) and John Mark (Acts 15:39).

Faith (1 Cor. 12:9)

The gift of faith is the ability to envision what needs to be done and to trust God to accomplish it even though it seems impossible to most people. Those with the gift of faith have a strong sense that God is going to accomplish something important through them or their ministry whether others see it as significant or not. They take Romans 8:28 literally and view obstacles as opportunities for Christ to accomplish his purposes in this world. They trust God in difficult, even impossible situations when others are ready to give up. This gift may cluster with the gift of leadership and can be found in some visionary Christians who dream big dreams, pray big prayers, and attempt big things for the Savior (Eph. 3:20).

Scripture presents several examples of people with great faith. In the Old Testament, Caleb and Joshua were men of unusual faith who led Israel in conquering and possessing the Promised Land. Nehemiah demonstrated his faith when he approached a hostile, pagan king and dared to ask permission to rebuild Jerusalem. The poor widow in Luke 21:2–4 showed great faith when she put practically all she had (two small copper coins) in the temple treasury for God. In the New Testament, God may have given Stephen the spiritual gift of faith, for Luke describes him as "a man full of faith" (Acts 6:5).

Giving (Rom. 12:8)

The gift of giving is the ability to give eagerly, wisely, generously, and sacrificially to others. Regardless of the amount, people with this gift genuinely view their treasures, talents, and time as on loan from God and not their own. They find that God moves them to give to those with genuine needs. They take special delight in giving of themselves and what they have to others. Tabitha may have exercised the gift of giving, for Luke describes her as "always doing good and helping the poor"(Acts 9:36). It is also possible that some in the church at Philippi ministered to Paul through the gift of giving (Phil. 4:14–18).

Helps (1 Cor. 12:28) and Service (Rom. 12:7)

These two gifts appear to be the same gift and involve the capacity to recognize and provide assistance in meeting practical needs, thus making life a little easier for others. It often concerns sacrificial, behind-the-scenes assistance and benefits others by freeing them up for vital ministries. People with these gifts were needed in Acts 6:1, where there was a dispute in the early church over its failure to serve the Hebraic widows. Phoebe probably exercised the gift of helps/service, according to Romans 16:1. Onesiphorus may have exercised this gift in Paul's life (2 Tim. 1:16), as did the household of Stephanas (1 Cor. 16:15). The term *deacon* is a form of the word for *service* (1 Tim. 3:8), and so those who are attracted to the office of deacon may have the spiritual gift of helps/service.

Leading (Rom. 12:8)

The gift of leadership is found in people who have a clear, significant vision and are able to communicate it publicly or privately in such a way that they influence others to pursue that vision. They tend to gravitate toward the "point position" in a particular ministry and lead in such a way that others have trust and confidence in them and their abilities. This gift is not to be confused with the gift of administration (1 Cor. 12:28).

Scripture is replete with examples of those with leadership abilities. In the Old Testament, God used people such as Abraham, Moses, Joshua, Caleb, David, Daniel, Nehemiah, and certain judges and kings to lead his people. The Gospels present the most outstanding example and model of leadership in the Savior. In the New Testament, other outstanding people who most likely had the spiritual gift of leadership were Paul, Peter, and James.

Mercy (Rom. 12:8)

The gift of mercy is the capacity to feel and express unusual compassion and sympathy for those in difficult or crisis situations and to provide them with the necessary help and support to see them through these times. They have the ability to "walk in another's shoes" and to feel the pain and burdens they carry. They do not stop there, however, but desire to embrace and make a difference in hurting people's lives for the Savior. Barnabas may have had this gift, as demonstrated by the mercy he extended to Paul in Acts 9:26–27, when he took him in and defended him before the other disciples. Dorcas may have also exercised the gift of mercy because she "was always doing good and helping the poor" (Acts 9:36).

Pastoring (Eph. 4:11)

The term *pastor* literally means shepherd. Therefore, based on the function of a Palestinian shepherd, the gift involves leading, nurturing, caring for, and protecting God's flock. This gift is commonly associated with those who minister professionally in the church in the position of pastor. However, God bestows the gift of pastor on lay people as well, including women. In fact, most of the pastoral care in the church can and should be the ministry of lay people. The recent biblical emphasis on small groups encourages this ministry, as lay-led groups provide an excellent context in which pastoral care may take place.

Some argue that the gift of pastor is to be associated with the gift of teacher, according to Ephesians 4:11. They believe two aspects or dimensions are combined in one gift. Thus someone with the gift of pastoring will have the gift of teaching, while the opposite may not be true. Though it is possible these gifts could cluster together (as is possible for any of the spiritual gifts), the original language does not demand it in Ephesians 4:11.[6]

In light of their function, the gift of pastor would be important to those occupying the position of elder in the church. In Acts 20:28 Paul instructs the elders in the church at Ephesus to "be shepherds of the church of God." In 1 Peter 5:2, Peter exhorts elders to "be shepherds of God's flock that is under your care."

Teaching (Rom. 12:7; 1 Cor. 12:28; Eph. 4:11)

The gift of teaching is the God-given ability to understand and communicate biblical truth. As stated earlier, it is not simply the ability to teach any truth, because God gives non-Christians the ability to teach general truth in areas such as business, medicine, computers, or music. Good teaching, however, does not merely involve the communication of Bible content but focuses on the insight it brings, and its relevance and application to the lives of the hearers.

The importance of teaching is obvious in the New Testament. In James 3:1 Jesus' half brother warns those who would be teachers of the grave responsibility of their teaching position. In Hebrews 5:12 the writer uses teaching as a litmus test of spiritual maturity. In 1 Timothy 5:17 certain elders are not only responsible to lead the church but also to preach to and teach the church.

Passion

Discerning your design for ministry also involves discerning your passion. It is the second piece to your life's puzzle. In Romans 15:20 Paul uses the term *ambition* to describe his passion to proclaim the gospel to the Gentiles. But what precisely is a person's passion or ambition? Why is it important? Are there any good examples in the Bible?

The Definition of Passion

Passion is a God-given capacity to fervently attach ourselves to an object (people, a cause, an idea, an area of ministry) over an extended period of time to meet a need. Several elements make up this definition.

Fervency

Passion involves fervency. Its emphasis is on feelings. It is "a burning desire—even to the point of being irrational."[7] Others have described it as a "burning feeling deep in your soul" or as a "burning gut-feeling that a certain ministry is the most important place that God would have you."

Object

Passion has an object. We say that a person has a passion for or toward someone or something. Thus it serves to focus our spiritual gifts. It may include people: the lost, unchurched, unborn, poor and oppressed, or unreached peoples. Paul had a passion toward the Gentiles, and Peter toward the Jews (Gal. 2:7). It could include a cause or an issue, such as abortion, civil rights, women's rights, the gospel, the clarity of the gospel, or the family. It could be a situation or condition, such as poverty, oppression, abuse, addiction, dysfunction, or legalism. It might be a particular pursuit, such as theology, preaching, or teaching. It might include a place, such as an urban, suburban, or rural area or possibly a specific city, state, or country.

Tenure

Passion has tenure; it stays with you for an extended period of time. We must be careful to distinguish between passion and passing interests. Passion "sticks to the bones"; passing interests come and go: Paul writes, "It has always been my ambition to preach the gospel . . ." (Rom. 15:20). Some who are involved in a particular ministry acknowledge that they have wanted to be in that ministry for as long as they can remember. That is the tenure of passion.

Need

Passion often develops out of a strong sense of felt need. This need has a way of capturing our attention and pressing in on our hearts. Thus it prompts the exercise of our gifts. It may involve our own needs, the needs of others, or both. God used Chuck Colson's prison experience to impress on him the needs of those behind bars. God used the oppressive racial milieu in Mississippi to prompt John Perkins to pursue the Voice of Calvary Ministry.

The Importance of Passion

While our spiritual gifts supply us with the tools or special abilities for our trade, our passion focuses and motivates those spiritual gifts.

Focus

Passion provides us with the necessary direction for ministry in general and for spiritual gifts in particular. Thus it serves to focus our ministry. Three people may have the gift of evangelism. One may have a passion for children, another for students on college campuses, and the third for Asian people. The first could exercise his or her evangelistic gift with Child Evangelism, Inc. The second could minister with Campus Crusade for Christ. The third could consider the mission field in the Orient or the ministry of International Students in America.

Motivation

Passion also provides us with the necessary motivation to exercise our gifts. It has a way of catalyzing or energizing us. It pushes and pulls us outside our comfort zones. It compels us to take some definite action. It spurs us to activity. It builds a fire in our soul that is only quenched momentarily by ministry activity.

Some Examples of Passion

The apostle Paul provides an example of passion. His passion was to preach the gospel to the Gentiles (the unchurched of the first century). He discovered his passion rather quickly (Acts 9:6, 15) but refined and sharpened it over an extended period of time. Initially his passion was to preach the gospel (1 Cor. 9:16–23) to both the Jews and the Gentiles (Acts 9:15; Rom. 9:1–3; 10:1). However, due to the rejection of the Jews, he later focused exclusively on the Gentiles (Acts 22:21; 26:17; Rom. 1:5; 11:13). This was further refined to preaching the gospel to Gentiles in places where Christ was not known (Rom. 15:20–21).

In his book *Honest to God?* Bill Hybels gives several examples of men and their passions. One is Dr. James Dobson, founder of Focus on the Family Ministries, who obviously has a powerful passion for the family. Another is international evangelist Luis Palau, who has a passion for the lost in general. A third is John Perkins, founder of the Voice of Calvary Ministries, who has a strong passion for the poor and needy minorities in the inner city. Finally there is R. C. Sproul, a reformed theologian and author, with a passion "to study and teach the very deepest truths of the Christian faith."[8]

Temperament

Discerning your divine design includes understanding your temperament. God-given spiritual gifts provide the special abilities for our ministries, and a God-given passion supplies long-term direction and motivation for those abilities. However, God-given temperament provides the unique personal characteristics and tendencies for ministry. Temperament is another vital piece of the puzzle. But what is temperament? Why is it important?

The Definition of Temperament

A careful reading of the general literature on human development and psychology reveals that often the terms *temperament* and *personality* are used synonymously. Consequently any definition of temperament must also comment on its relationship to the concept of personality. An examination of the two terms indicates that a distinction exists. While there is difference of opinion among those in the field of human development, Hughes and Noppe indicate that a person's temperament is the foundation and forerunner for his or her personality.[9] They view temperament as a predisposition and precursor that contributes to our future personality makeup and its development.

If a person's temperament contributes to personality, then what is a definition of temperament? I define temperament as your unique, God-given (inborn) behavioral style. Hughes and Noppe define temperament as a person's "inborn behavioral characteristics."[10] The term *inborn* implies that the temperament characteristics were present at birth. In *Parenting Isn't for Cowards* James Dobson writes, "It is my supposition that these temperaments are pre-packaged before birth and do not have to be cultivated or encouraged."[11] From birth it is evident that people have certain God-given behavioral characteristics already in place that are basic and unique to their makeup. It is possible that this is what Jeremiah is referring to in Jeremiah 1:5 and Paul in Galatians 1:15.

Next, temperament concerns behavior. In general, temperament is based on a person's actions or behavioral style. Each person has a unique behavioral pattern or style that involves a distinct way of thinking, feeling, and acting. This behavior can be motivated by a person's needs or values. The former affects how a person acts, the latter why a person acts the way he does. Most temperament tools concern needs-motivated behavior.

Finally, temperament focuses on a person's inborn behavioral characteristics such as intelligence, initiative, self-assurance, and scholarship. Various terms are used besides *characteristics,* such as *tendencies* or *traits.* Regardless of the exact term, these inborn traits determine similarities and differences in the behavior of people. Ultimately the various organizations of these common traits constitute a person's individual temperament. In general these temperament characteristics remain constant over a period of time and are not permanently altered by temporary pressures from one's environment.

The Importance of Temperament

A knowledge of temperament is important for a variety of reasons.

First we can learn a great deal about ourselves and others when we explore the various temperaments and their behavioral types. While the Bible does not directly define temperament or personality, this concept serves as a convenient and helpful way to understand and describe the personal characteristics and tendencies of Christians and non-Christians that influence their thoughts, emotions, and ultimately their behavior.

Second, ministry involves working with all kinds of different people and behavioral styles. By identifying our behavioral styles and the styles of others, we have the potential to increase ministry effectiveness. This directly affects our servanthood. When we understand another Christian's temperament, we are better able to serve him or her (Mark 9:35; 10:43; Phil. 2:3–8).

Third, we must understand that people are different in fundamental ways, and that is okay. They have different wants, needs, motives, desires, goals, and values. The problem is not these differences but that we account for them in destructive ways. Our tendency is to see the differences in others as flaws, especially where they differ from us. We want to change people and make them more like us. The results can be disastrous in marriage, family, or team ministry.

The Description of Temperament

A number of different temperament models have surfaced in the past few years. Most of them derive from one of two prototypes.

The first is based on the traditional four-temperament model developed by Hippocrates 2,000 years ago. He believed a person's temperament was based on the mixture of various fluids such as blood and bile in the human body. He named the four temperaments choleric, sanguine, melancholic, and phlegmatic.

The Personal Profile is based on the four-temperament model and is growing in popularity in the marketplace and with many Christian organizations. It was developed by John G. Geier and Dorothy E. Downey and based on the earlier work of William Marston, who popularized the DiSC model. DiSC is an acronym for the four behavioral temperaments: Dominant, Influencing, Steady, and Compliant. These are further broken down into fifteen profile patterns.

Another useful tool is the Biblical Personal Profile developed by Ken Voges. It uses the same terminology and methodology as the Personal Profile but applies the profiles to biblical characters in the interpretative stage.

Both tools allow individuals to analyze their behavior in nine specific categories:

1. Emotional tendencies
2. Goals
3. The criteria used in judging others
4. The means used to influence others
5. The perceived value one has to an organization
6. The tendency one has to overuse certain traits
7. The typical reaction under pressure
8. Fears
9. What one needs to do to increase personal effectiveness[12]

The other prototype is the Myers-Briggs Type Indicator (MBTI). It has become the most widely used tool for the nonpsychiatric population in

America. It takes a different approach than the two profiles above in that it helps us discern our inborn preferences in four key functional areas of life.

First the MBTI seeks to determine our preference for extraversion or introversion. This helps in knowing where we focus our attention (the inner or outer world) and what energizes us: people or ideas.

Second the MBTI helps us discover how we perceive or take in information. We prefer either sensing, which involves receiving information through the five senses, or intuition, which gathers information intuitively or beyond the senses (a kind of sixth sense). People characterized by the former see things with their eyes and tend to be less visionary; the latter see things in their heads and are the world's visionaries.

Third the MBTI helps us discover how we process the information we take in or how we make decisions. This involves a preference for thinking or feeling. These terms can be misleading. Those who prefer thinking make decisions based on logic and objective analysis; whereas those who prefer feeling make decisions based more on personal values and judgments. This does not mean that the former do not have values, or that the latter do not think, as might be implied from the terms.

Finally the MBTI helps in determining the lifestyle we adopt for dealing with the outer world. This involves a preference for judging or perceiving. Again the terms can be confusing. Those who prefer judging are not judgmental people but prefer to take a planned, organized approach to life. They like closure and are quick decision makers. People who prefer perceiving are adaptable and take a spontaneous, flexible approach to life. They do not like closure, preferring to wait until all the information is in before making a final decision.[13]

Some Examples of Temperament

Bill Hybels gives several examples of the impact of temperament on certain men and their ministries. James Dobson is an extroverted, relational man who deeply cares about this country, its people, and their needs. He is people-oriented. This puts his radio guests at ease and draws the interest of listeners around the world, especially those in struggling families. Luis Palau is an excitable, fiery person whose vision, focus, and intensity attract an audience and their undivided attention. R. C. Sproul, while an excellent communicator in front of an audience, is task-oriented and prefers being by himself for hours in his study, thinking and doing research. Finally John Perkins is a quiet, gentle, feeling kind of man. Hybels writes, "He just slips in and fits in with the group. Certainly that's one of the keys to his success in working with the downtrodden. His temperament is gentle enough to be nonthreatening and encouraging."[14] Hybels himself is an extrovert who is energized by being around people. He is a visionary (an intuitive) who saw Willow Creek Community Church in his head long before he planted it. He is also an "off the charts thinker" who is relatively unstructured, which is important in church planting.[15]

The Theological Justification for Temperament

Christians should be hesitant to use or be assessed with tools that might be influenced by so-called modern psychological principles. These principles could be based on unbiblical presuppositions. The question is, Do temperament tools such as the Personal Profile and the Myers-Briggs Temperament Inventory fall in this category?

General and Special Revelation

Evangelical theologians recognize two domains of revelation. One is special revelation, which refers to God's knowledge as found in Christ (John 1:18) and the Scriptures (1 John 5:9–12). The other is general revelation, which refers to God's knowledge as found in his creation: nature, science, and history. The former is the domain of the theologian; the latter is the domain of both the scientist and the theologian. Christians have no problems with knowledge based on the former. Most accept the Bible as God's trustworthy, authoritative word. The problem lies in knowledge based on general revelation—it may or may not be compatible with Scripture. Psychological and temperament tests fall under the category of general revelation.

All Truth Is God's Truth

While all the content of the Bible is true (2 Tim. 3:16), not all truth is found in the Bible. For example, scientists have discovered the truth that if people brush and floss their teeth on a regular basis, they will have fewer cavities. They have also found that cigarette smoking is harmful to your health. Both truths are not found in the Bible, yet few would challenge their validity. I could cite numerous other examples. The point is that all truth is ultimately God's truth. The problem lies in discerning truth from error in the domain of general revelation. When Scripture addresses a topic, we have God's truth on the matter. But how do we discern God's truth in matters that Scripture does not address, such as the brushing and flossing of our teeth, smoking cigarettes, or matters of temperament? When dealing with knowledge based on general revelation, the Christian must proceed cautiously.

The key to the truthfulness of any temperament or psychological profile is its degree of accuracy in correctly detecting behavioral styles. Those that prove accurate over time are most likely based ultimately on God's truth regardless of their source, but those that do not prove accurate are not based on divine truth. Consequently the validation of a temperament tool is important to the Christian who is seeking God's truth in the domain of natural revelation.[16]

Both the Biblical and Personal Profiles and the Myers-Briggs Temperament Inventory have demonstrated high reliability, as based on professional studies of their validity. The Personal Profile has been through a rigid validation process, and the results are available in *The Kaplan Report*.[17] Katharine Briggs and Isabel Myers as well as others have submitted the MBTI to rigorous standards of validity.[18] That is why it is used so widely today in the nonpsychiatric population. Those of us who have worked with these tools over the years have found from personal experience that they accurately detect behavioral styles.

Wisdom Tradition

The Old Testament contains several books classified as Hebrew wisdom literature. The books are Proverbs, Job, Ecclesiastes, and certain psalms that deal specifically with the topic of wisdom.[19] The Hebrew concept of wisdom was essentially practical. They did not distinguish between the intellectual and the practical or the religious and the secular. For them the whole of life was to be viewed from the religious experience, and wisdom was relevant to every area of man's existence.[20]

According to scholars biblical wisdom literature reflects more influence from the ancient Near East than the other literature in the Bible. Harrison writes, "It would seem clear, therefore, that not merely was Hebrew wisdom far from being an isolated literary or didactic phenomenon, but that in fact it was part of a large cultural heritage common to the whole of the ancient world."[21] However, Harrison is careful to point out that the Hebrew writers did not depend entirely on other ancient Near Eastern wisdom sources for their contribution.[22] In his commentary on Proverbs, Derek Kidner adds that parallels with the Book of Proverbs show that Israel's wise men sifted through and assimilated some of the wisdom tradition of the Near East.[23]

David Ward explains this process and how it interacts with inspiration:

> Under divine inspiration, Solomon and others sometimes took wise lessons from life captured in proverbs composed by pagan wise men, and reoriented their advice under the proper frame of reference. Namely, the fear of the Lord. Wisdom living had more to do with successful living in this world than it did with any redemptive vision of a future heaven. Therefore when wise insight was seen to help live for the true God more effectively, it was adopted as God's truth anyway. So it was not as much a case of being unoriginal and borrowing as it was a case of recovering truth for the believer's use that was God's truth in the first place.[24]

The point is that God's inerrant, authoritative Word under divine inspiration drew on lessons of truth and wisdom from the surrounding cultures. Again, the reason is that all truth is God's truth regardless of where it is found. Consequently the careful use of insights from validated, reliable temperament tools closely parallels the wisdom process of Israel's sages.

Temperament and Spiritual Gifts

Some excellent work is being done in discovering how the spiritual gifts combine with the various temperaments, especially the traditional, four-temperament model represented by the Personal Profile (DiSC) and the Biblical Personal Profile. For example, the gift of teaching will function differently with the various temperaments. Those who combine the high D temperament (strong, direct, confident) with the gift of teaching are highly dedicated teachers who will strongly challenge students. However, they will need to work hard at relating to their students on a personal level.

The high I temperament (influential, expressive, enthusiastic, persuasive) with the gift of teaching will inspire students and influence them.

These people are very articulate and prove to be excellent communicators. However, they can oversell their ideas and be manipulative.

The high S temperament (steady, dependable, relational) with the teaching gift tends to be a specialist who is consistent and works well with students. However, such teachers do not respond well to conflict in the classroom and people who differ with them or challenge their ideas.

Finally, those with the high C temperament (logical, persistent, conscientious) and the gift of teaching are methodical, analytical, and thorough. They highly value scholarship and may be scholars themselves. It is important to them that they be correct, and they like to develop methods to help people approach a particular discipline. However, they can become too detailed and picky.[25] In chapter 4 you will discover what your temperament is.

Leadership

Discerning your divine design involves discovering your leadership abilities. Christian leaders are godly people (character) who know where they are going (vision) and have followers (influence). Determining your ability to lead involves two primary areas: your leadership role and your leadership style. Both are important pieces of the design puzzle.

Leadership Roles

Determining your leadership role involves discovering whether you are a leader or a manager or a combination of both. Leadership is fundamentally different from management or administration.[26] Scripture makes a distinction between the gift of leadership (Rom. 12:8) and the gift of administration (1 Cor. 12:28). Many students of leadership make the same distinction. In the *Harvard Business Review* John Kotter writes that "Leadership is different from management, but not for the reasons most people think." He explains that "leadership and management are two distinctive and complementary systems of action. Each has its own function and characteristic activities."[27] Writers such as Ted Engstrom, Abraham Zaleznik, Bruce Jones, Mary Tramel, Helen Reynolds, and others also recognize this distinction.[28]

Leaders

In the 1990s tremendous change (megachange) is sweeping across North America. It will continue into the twenty-first century and will make an impact on everything in its path, including church and parachurch ministries. A characteristic of good leadership is the ability to cope with the change that comes from outside the organization and channel it to create needed change within the ministry organization.[29] The result is that Christian ministries relate relevantly, effectively, and biblically to their contemporary culture.

The way leaders cope with and accomplish change is through influence. Leadership involves influencing people to change in the direction of maximum Christlikeness and ministry effectiveness.

How do leaders influence people? The answer is found in the definition of a Christian leader. I have defined Christian leaders as godly people who know where they are going and have followers. Leaders who have followers exert influence. If no one is following your leadership, then you have little or no influence. The key to influence is the first two aspects of leadership: godliness (character) and direction (vision). People with godly, Christlike character attract followers. Visionary people who know and are excited about where they are going in life also attract followers. And when character and vision combine in one person, that leader exerts a powerful influence over others.

In addition, leaders are adept at developing vision and strategies for their ministries and motivating people to accomplish those visions through their strategies. They are visionaries who tend to think inductively more than deductively. They are also more proactive than reactive, and many have both the spiritual and natural gift of leadership.

Managers

Managers complement and work best under leaders by coping with the complexity of change. In fact, a major distinction between the role of leaders and managers is that while the former cope with change, the latter deal with the complexity that change brings.[30] Managers or administrators attempt to bring order and consistency to this complexity.

In *Leaders*, Bennis and Nanus see another distinction between leaders and managers. They write, "*Managers are people who do things right and leaders are people who do the right thing.* The difference may be summarized as activities of vision and judgment—*effectiveness* versus activities of mastering routines—*efficiency.*"[31] The distinction may be that leaders exercise leadership functions intuitively. In the process of ministry, they naturally do things right. Similarly in the *Effective Executive*, Peter Drucker addresses the difference between effectiveness and efficiency in organizations. Effectiveness is the ability to get the right things done; whereas efficiency is the ability to do things right.[32] Leaders intuitively tend toward the former, managers the latter.

Managers bring order and consistency to the complexity of change through such activities as planning, budgeting, and organizing. In fact, managers are godly people (character) who help us to get where we are going (plan) and maximize our resources to get there (budgeting, organizing, staffing, controlling). Managers think more deductively than inductively. Often they are also more reactive than proactive, and may have the spiritual and natural gifts of administration (1 Cor. 12:28).

Leaders and Managers

Though a person can be a pure leader or manager, most tend to rest somewhere along a continuum between the two. A Christian could be primarily a leader with some administrative abilities or vice versa (see figure 3). Peter Wagner agrees:

> Few pastors are pure leaders and administrators. Most are a mix of the two. But I have observed that pastors who tend toward being leaders, whether or not they are also administrators, will most likely be church growth pastors. Pastors who see themselves to be administrators and use that kind of management style tend to be maintenance-oriented. Making sure that the church functions smoothly and harmoniously is usually where a manager is. A leader, on the other hand, is willing to take risks and upset the status quo in order to move out toward new horizons.[33]

In *Leaders*, Bennis and Nanus studied ninety top leaders in an attempt to discover what it takes to be an effective leader as well as a manager. One interesting conclusion is that most organizations are overmanaged and underled. I would argue that this is true of most churches in North America as well.

The Leader-Manager Roles

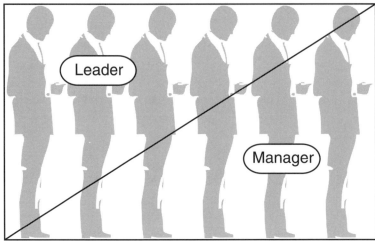

Figure 3

Leadership Styles

Once you have discerned whether you are more a leader or a manager or, most likely, some combination of the two with one more dominant than the other, the next step is to identify your leadership style. Four leadership styles exist that correspond to the four DiSC profiles. In their book *Understanding How Others Misunderstand You,* Voges and Braund succinctly identify and summarize these four styles under the terms *autocratic, democratic, participatory,* and *bureaucratic.* Though some of these terms may have positive connotations *(democratic, participatory)* or negative connotations *(autocratic, bureaucratic),* they are all used here in a *positive* sense in the context of God's design. All four styles are good and vital to the body of Christ.

The Autocratic Style

The autocratic style is characteristic of the high D temperament. As leaders they are catalytic self-starters who love a challenge and expect immediate results. They are decision makers who are quick to take authority and are good at managing trouble and solving problems.[34] If these leaders are in charge, Voges and Braund write, "An hierarchy of leadership is installed so that there is a direct line of authority."[35]

In *Ministerial Leadership in a Managerial World*, Bruce Jones refers to this as essentially a dominant style and says, "Pastors with these tendencies want to take charge of their environment to bring about needed change. They will be more highly task-oriented."[36]

The Democratic Style

The democratic style is characteristic of the high I temperament. High I leaders are enthusiastic people who enjoy being around and motivating people. They make favorable impressions and are usually articulate. They enjoy helping others and prefer to minister in teams.[37] Voges and Braund comment, "The influencing leader usually prefers to have the authority to make the final decision after representative views are expressed."[38]

Jones refers to this style with the term *influencing*. He writes, "These pastors are much more people-oriented and want to bring about change by stimulating and facilitating others to action. They are usually very warm in their relationships and possess good verbal and social skills."[39]

The Participatory Style

The participatory style is characteristic of the high S temperament. As leaders, they are patient people who are good at listening and calming down excited people. They are also loyal, focused, and cooperative.[40] Voges and Braund note that "Most of the daily decisions are delegated to others while the high S leader offers support by listening to others and allowing everyone in the organization the opportunity to follow through on individual assignments. This facilitating leader strives for peace and smooth operation in the company."[41]

Jones essentially calls this a steadiness style. He writes, "These pastors tend to major on stability and maintenance of traditions. They are usually loyal, patient, and supportive of others."[42]

The Bureaucratic Style

The bureaucratic style is characteristic of the high C temperament. High C leaders are analytical people who pay close attention to key directives, standards, and details. They are critical thinkers who check for accuracy and comply with authority.[43] Voges and Braund observe that "As long as there is compliance to policies, people in the organization can have their own responsibilities and make their own decisions. The organizational system and not personality style tends to be in charge."[44]

Jones uses the term *compliance* in describing the high C pastoral leader. He writes, "These pastors are very conscientious, attentive to detail, and concerned about rules, regulations, and order. They work systematically and are often sensitive and intuitive."[45]

It is possible that a Christian could be a pure high D or I or S or C leader. However, it is more likely that leaders will express a combination of two of these styles with one dominating the other.

Evangelism

Discerning your divine makeup also includes discovering your evangelism style. It is an often ignored yet important piece of your life's puzzle. When most Christians, including many in vocational ministry, hear the term *evangelism*, they associate it with a confrontational style only. They picture the stereotypical evangelist with raised Bible in hand cornering some defenseless soul and shouting at the top of his lungs, "Repent!" They conclude that evangelism is not for them and avoid it all together.

Confrontational evangelism is a valid style and has resulted in a number of people coming to faith in the Savior. However, it is not for everyone. In *Honest to God?* Bill Hybels writes:

> Only a tiny fraction of unbelievers in this world will be reached by the stereotypical evangelist. The unbelieving world is made up of a variety of people: young and old, rich and poor, educated and uneducated, urban and rural, with different races, personalities, values, political systems, and religious backgrounds. Isn't it obvious it would take more than one style of evangelist to reach such a diverse population?

> That's where we come in. Somewhere in that multifarious group is a person who needs to hear the message of Christ from someone just like you or me. A person who needs an evangelist of your exact age, career, and level of spiritual understanding, or my exact personality, background, and interests.[46]

Then Hybels points to six evangelistic styles: confrontational, intellectual, testimonial, relational, invitational, and serving.

The Confrontational Style

The confrontational style is illustrated by Peter in Acts 2. Peter confronts more than 3,000 Jews with the truth that "you, with the help of wicked men, put him to death" (Acts 2:23). And later in verse 36 he says, "Therefore let all Israel be assured of this: God has made this Jesus, whom you crucified, both Lord and Christ." Peter witnesses unabashedly to this large group of the horror of what they have done, with little concern as to how his hearers might react. Peter's style may be described as confident, controversial, challenging, frontal, courageous, and straightforward.

After commenting on Peter's style and approach, Hybels, himself a confrontational style evangelist, writes, "Some people will only come to Christ if they are 'knocked over the head with truth' and confronted by someone like Peter. Fortunately, God has equipped certain believers with the combination of personality, gifts, and desires that make it natural for them to confront others."[47]

The Intellectual Style

The intellectual style is illustrated by Paul in Acts 17. The setting is a Jewish synagogue in Thessalonica. Paul entered the synagogue and "reasoned with them from the Scriptures, explaining and proving that the Christ had to suffer and rise from the dead" (vv. 2–3). Later in Athens (vv. 16–17), Paul again "reasoned in the synagogue with the Jews and the God-fearing Greeks." The same characterized his sermon to the Athenian philosophers on Mars Hill (vv. 18–31). Paul's style is best described as educated, intelligent, cogent, well-reasoned, logical, and accurate.

Regarding the intellectual style, Hybels asks, "What about you? Could you be an intellectual evangelist? Are you an effective debater? Do you enjoy examining evidence and reasoning through to a conclusion? Do you like to wrestle with difficult questions? Do you love it when cultists come to your door? Then take your calling as an intellectual evangelist seriously. Read, study, and train yourself."[48]

The Testimonial Style

The testimonial style is illustrated by the story of the healing of the beggar in John 9. Jesus healed a blind man on the Sabbath, which caused a split among the Pharisees—some thought he was a sinner, others thought he was from God. When the former asked the healed man what he thought about Jesus, he responded with a testimonial: "Whether he is a sinner or not, I don't know. One thing I do know. I was blind but now I see!" (v. 25). This style is excited, confident, firm, personal, biographical, straightforward, honest, concise, and powerful. These people have a personal story to tell of how Christ has made a difference in their lives, and they tell practically everyone who will listen.

Hybels writes, "Testimonial style evangelists neither confront nor intellectualize. They simply tell the story of the miraculous work of Christ in their life. They say, 'I was spiritually blind, but now I see. Jesus Christ changed my life, and He can change yours.'"[49] This can take place between two men over lunch, across two neighbors' back fence, or between several housewives waiting for their children after school.

The Relational Style

The relational style is illustrated by the account of the demon-possessed man in Mark 5 who lived among the tombs. Jesus met him and cast the demons out. As a result of what Christ had done, the man begged the Savior to take him along on his ministry travels (5:18). Mark states that, "Jesus did not let him, but said, 'Go home to your family and tell them how much the Lord has done for you, and how he has had mercy on you'" (5:19). This style is highly personal, family-oriented, emotional, patient, passionate, and local.

Hybels adds, "Jesus, in effect, said, 'Don't go knocking on doors, doing "cold-turkey" evangelism with people you don't even know. You have family and friends who need to know what I have done in your life. Go home and live a transformed life in their presence. Diligently pray for them, then wait for divinely appointed opportunities to tell your story. Be available when someone says, "How can I get what you have?"'"[50]

The Invitational Style

The invitational style is illustrated by the story of the Samaritan woman in John 4. Jesus encountered a promiscuous woman of Samaria and after an extended conversation presented himself as Messiah (vv. 25–26). In her excitement she left her waterpots, returned to her town, and invited all her people to "Come, see a man who told me everything I ever did. Could this be the Christ?" (v. 29). The result is found in verse 39: "Many of the Samaritans from that town believed in him because of the woman's testimony, 'He told me everything I ever did.'" This style is somewhat persuasive, persistent, opportunistic, and effective for those who are not good at articulating their faith.

Hybels describes the woman's evangelistic style: "The Samaritan woman was an invitational evangelist. She knew she wasn't prepared to articulate the message in a powerful way. So she invited her friends and acquaintances to come and hear someone who could explain it more effectively."[51] Then Hybels illustrates from his own ministry: "I estimate that fifty percent of the people who write and tell me about their conversion experience say something like this: 'I was lost. I was confused. I was lonely. Then someone invited me to a Sunday service—or to a concert, a holiday service, a special event. I kept coming back, and over time I came to know Christ in a personal way.'"[52]

The Serving Style

The serving style is illustrated by Dorcas in Acts 9. Scripture describes her as a disciple, "who was always doing good and helping the poor" (v. 36). Apparently she spent a great deal of her time serving other people in various ways not detailed in the text. She also had a great impact on the poor. This style is characterized by care, tenderness, compassion, love, patience, energy, hospitality, service, and quiet strength.

Hybels comments, "Dorcas was a service evangelist. She used her unique serving gifts as tangible expressions of the Gospel message. Like her, you may have a tender spirit and helpful heart. You may have gifts of mercy, helps, hospitality, giving, and counseling. You may be very effective evangelists as you connect sharing Christ with serving people."[53]

There are numbers of ways to evangelize through serving. We can mow a neighbor's grass while he is out of town or take food to one who is an invalid. We can help a coworker repair his automobile or provide a ride to work when his vehicle is in the shop.

The six styles of evangelism serve only to introduce us to the concept of discovering our natural, personal style. As many styles exist as there are different kinds of Christians. A more thorough study of the Scriptures, especially the biographical portions, reveals other styles as well. A Christian may have several styles of evangelism. Paul not only displayed an intellectual style but also a confrontational style (Acts 13:46; 14:3; 16:18). Both the invitational and testimonial styles are found in the Samaritan woman (compare John 4:29 with 4:39).

Natural Gifts and Talents

Discerning God's design involves discovering your natural gifts and talents. They are a more obvious component of your design from God and provide another missing piece of the puzzle. What are natural gifts and talents? They are abilities that God distributes to all people regardless of their spiritual condition for the benefit of all humankind. We will look at their source, essence, and recipients.

The Source of Natural Gifts

Natural gifts, like spiritual gifts, are from God. As the Master Creator and Designer, God delegates to each person certain talents and gifts. Unlike spiritual gifts, however, which are given at conversion, natural gifts are in place at birth. In fact, in some children they may manifest themselves at an early age, as seen in the child who teaches himself to play the piano, or paints extraordinarily well, or has the ability to multiply large numbers in her head.

The Essence of Natural Gifts

Natural gifts and talents are abilities or capabilities. Many spiritual gifts have corresponding natural gifts. Unbelievers have natural abilities to lead, administer, give, encourage, show mercy, help, trust, teach, but they cannot have spiritual insight. When a natural and spiritual gift combine in one person, a believer can exert a powerful impact in ministry.

Natural gifts may have little if anything in common with spiritual gifts. I am referring to such talents as the ability to write, draw, sing, play a musical instrument, participate in sports, analyze a problem, design objects, conceive ideas, persuade people, and many others.

The Recipients of Natural Gifts

God has given talents and gifts to all people, not just Christians. Natural observation and experience as well as history tell us that unbelievers are just as talented and gifted as believers. Natural gifts and talents are for the good of all, an aspect of God's common grace whereby he blesses everyone on the basis of his goodness and benevolence and not their personal worth or merit. People without Christ are totally depraved, yet because of God's common grace they are not totally forgotten.

Other Components

I call the previous six components—spiritual gifts, passion, temperament, leadership role and style, evangelism style, and natural gifts and talents— the primary areas of design assessment. However, there are additional design components. I will briefly mention five.[54]

One is your style of spiritual growth. Numerous books have been written on how to attain spiritual maturity, and most prescribe a method or rules for all to follow regardless of how God has "wired" them. Mattson and Miller have a different perspective:

> The kinds of techniques that are embraced for the sake of spiritual discipline need to be individual. A set of rules made to discipline a person who has one motivational pattern may actually encourage unsanctified expression of another's pattern.
>
> Scripture does not outline one specific, step-by-step program aimed at maturing all Christians. Each individual requires a unique strategy. What one person needs will not work for another. What cripples one Christian

may be a sign of health in another. This is troubling to those who want Christians in a more standardized package. God, however, has made each of us unique and never tires of ministering to every need.[55]

Another component is your learning style. We tend to assume that others learn as we do. This simply is not the case. Just as we have different leadership and evangelism styles, so we have different learning styles. Educators have found at least four.[56] I believe that many more exist, and the same is true of the other design components below. Regardless, knowing your learning style is crucial to your own learning and teaching.[57]

A third component is your conflict management style. Norman Shaw-chuck recognizes at least five styles people use to resolve conflict.[58] A knowledge of your style and the ability to recognize the style of another could prove the difference between working harmoniously with another Christian and disaster.

A fourth component is your thinking style. Research indicates that people have a preferred style of thinking that falls in one of five areas.[59] At times we may use all of these styles or a combination of them.

A fifth component is your team-player style. Research has discovered that people who work together on a team display four styles.[60] Each team member's style contributes in different ways to the accomplishment of the team's goals and objectives. Each style also has a downside that can distract the team from realizing its vision. Since New Testament ministry is team ministry, Christians will benefit from discovering and implementing their team-player styles.[61]

Worksheet

1. Do you know how God has designed you for ministry? Why or why not?

2. How do you define a spiritual gift? Is your definition different from the one in this chapter? If yes, what is the difference? What is the difference between a natural and a spiritual gift?

3. What arguments would you give for the importance of spiritual gifts? Why might a person not want to identify his or her spiritual gifts? What is the difference between a gift-mix and a gift-cluster? Do you believe other gifts exist beyond those named in the Bible? Why or why not? If so, what gifts would you name?

4. What is the biblical justification for the concept of design-passion? Why is a person's passion important to his or her ministry design? Can you identify design-passions other than those mentioned in this chapter?

5. Why is your temperament important to your divine design? Is temperament a biblical concept? Does it have to be? Why or why not? Name several people in ministry other than those mentioned in this chapter and identify their temperaments. How do their temperaments help or hinder their ministries?

♦

6. What is your definition of a leader? Is it different from the definition in this chapter? If so, how? How important is influence to leadership? What is the key to influence?

7. What is the difference between role and style in leadership? Is there a difference between leadership and management or administration? If yes, what are some differences? Are some leadership styles in this chapter better or more right than others? Explain.

8. What is your natural reaction to confrontational evangelism? What might your reaction tell you about your style of evangelism? Is confrontational evangelism bad or good? Do other evangelistic styles exist besides the six covered in this chapter? Can you find others in the Bible?

The Discovery of Your Divine Design 4

Do You Know Who You Are?

Like Tom, David has begun to get some sleep at night. He submitted his resignation to the church board, and his nightmare as a pastor is about to end. He had applied to a seminary as a doctoral student and has been accepted. When the good news arrived in the mail, his heart leaped inside him—a sense of joy he had not experienced back when he was first voted in as the new pastor of this church. Of course, he knows things won't be easy.

He will be committed to the doctoral program for the next three years, and after that his future is still uncertain. Teaching positions in North America are few and far between, so he probably will teach on the foreign mission field. But he isn't concerned because for once he feels a sense of self-esteem and significance—he is about to accomplish what he really wants to do with his life.

What prompted this change of direction? One morning an alumni letter from the seminary interrupted his sermon study, offering an assessment package that would help interested graduates discover their place in ministry. It was titled: Discovering Your Personal Ministry Vision. A few minutes later David contacted the alumni director by phone, and the assessment package was on its way. It took David several weeks to complete the divine design discovery process, but when he was done he knew better who he was and why he had to risk a change of ministry.

What was the process that David worked through? How did he discover his personal ministry vision, and how can you? It began with discerning his personal design for ministry—the components described in chapter 3— spiritual gifts, passion, temperament, leadership role and style, evangelism style, and natural gifts and talents.

Discovering Your Spiritual Gifts

At this point, you realize you have several different spiritual gifts (a gift-mix), and you have a working description of most of the gifts in the Bible. The next step is to discover your spiritual gifts.

The Importance of Discovering Your Gifts

Interest in spiritual gifts has ebbed and flowed over the last half of the twentieth century. Is the attempt to discover our spiritual gifts simply another Christian fad, or is it biblical? The Scriptures teach that it is indeed important—for two reasons.

In 1 Timothy 4:12–16, Paul instructs Timothy to maintain his integrity and continue his preaching and teaching of the Bible, and then Paul concludes: "Be diligent in these matters; give yourself wholly to them, so that everyone may see your progress." In 2 Timothy 1:6 Paul instructs Timothy to "fan into flame the gift of God." Paul is exhorting Timothy to heavily involve himself in the exercise of his gift. Both passages assume that Timothy has identified his gift(s).

In 1 Corinthians 12:31, Paul concludes a discussion on spiritual gifts with this imperative: "But eagerly desire the greater gifts." In chapter 13, he then describes our highest pursuit—love for one another. Then in 14:1 Paul brings the two ideas together: "Follow the way of love and eagerly desire spiritual gifts." This raises two questions: How could they "eagerly desire" spiritual gifts if they didn't know what they were, and why should they desire them if they are not important?

The Process of Discovering Your Gifts

In my ministry I have found the following eight-step, gifts-discovery process to be most helpful: prayer, study, desire, analysis, experience, fulfillment, confirmation, and fruit.

Prayer

John Bunyan said, "You can do more than pray once you've prayed, but you cannot do more than pray until you have prayed." The place to start in discovering your gift-mix is prayer. Indeed, the entire process must be bathed in prayer.

Pray for wisdom and insight for your personal ministry in general and your spiritual gifts in particular. Ask God to reveal to you your gifts in whatever way he deems fit. At the same time, stay alert so that you do not miss any answers or opportunities he may send your way (Eph. 6:18).

This prayer must also be intentional. I suggest that you set aside a regular time each day for prayer and include specific requests for the identification of your gifts and abilities. The Savior set us an example, for according to Mark 1:35 he practiced the spiritual discipline of awaking early in the morning and traveling to a solitary place where he would pray without interruption. Whenever or however you do it is not as important as the fact that you do it.

Finally your prayer time is a good time for an integrity check. Periodically ask yourself, Why do I want to discover my design and spiritual gifts? What are my true motives? Am I doing this for God or myself? The correct motive is to glorify God, not ourselves. If there is a problem here, resolve it before you proceed.

Study

Another step in the process of discovering your gifts is to do a Bible study of the spiritual gifts. Turn in your Bible to the chapters on spiritual gifts (1 Cor. 12; Rom. 12; Eph. 4; and 1 Peter 4) and read and pray over the gifts listed in these chapters. Though Scripture is not crystal clear as to the meaning of all the gifts, attempt to discern the nature of each gift and how they were used.

In chapter 3 of this book I provided a list of spiritual gifts. At this point, return to that list and read over it carefully. Do you find yourself attracted to any of the gifts? If so, study those gifts in detail. Learn as much as possible about each one. Find someone with these gifts and learn what you can from them about their use.

This is a subjective approach to identifying your gifts and must be pursued carefully. The problem is you may select a gift based not on your actual abilities but your wishes. Some people wish for gifts and ministries that they and others admire but that are not true to who they are. Many Christians admire the ministry of Billy Graham and his gift of evangelism, and they want to be like him. However, they do not have his gifts and could waste much of their ministry attempting the ministry of evangelism.

Desire

A third step in the process is to examine your personal desires. Ask yourself, What do I really want to do? While this is highly subjective and could mislead you, as in the Billy Graham illustration above, it may lead to the discovery of your gifts. David says, "Delight yourself in the Lord and he will give you the desires of your heart" (Ps. 37:4). In *The Dynamics of Spiritual Gifts*, William McRae writes that, according to this passage, God places certain desires in the believer's heart.[1] Whether or not this passage is specifically teaching that God gives us certain desires, it does teach that God may honor the desires of our hearts. Consequently a specific desire to teach, evangelize, or show mercy could be from God or honored by God. Again we must examine the motives behind the desire.

Analysis

A fourth step in the discovery process is analysis. This is the objective side of the gifts discovery process that can serve to balance the subjective elements. It involves taking a spiritual gifts inventory. Many inventories are now available. I suggest that you take more than one, since each inventory has a slightly different format and approach.

Often the gifts inventories are divided into two groups. One consists of those that test for all the gifts, including the sign gifts, such as the Wagner-Modified Houts Questionnaire. The other group consists of inventories that exclude the sign gifts, such as the Houts Inventory of Spiritual Gifts or the Basden-Johnson Spiritual Gifts Analysis. I have listed some of the inventories available in appendix G.

I have provided the Spiritual Gifts Inventory for your use in appendix A. It is important to realize that you are the final judge of your gifts, not some inventory. For a variety of reasons, the Spiritual Gifts Inventory or any of the other inventories mentioned in this chapter may not accurately reflect your design. If you doubt the inventory results, retake it now and then again several months later. Now turn to the Spiritual Gifts Inventory in appendix A and complete it before you proceed.[2]

Experience

It is difficult if not impossible to discover your gifts while sitting around your dining room table at home or in a pew at church. If you are a student, it will be difficult to discern your gifts if you spend all your time in the school library or in the classroom (unless you have had several years of prior ministry experience). The process happens much faster and more accurately if we are "up to our elbows" in ministry. In *The Making of a Leader*, Bobby Clinton writes, "Gifts normally emerge in the context of small groups or when a leader has a ministry assignment. Most lay leaders will discover gifts by using them, without recognizing that they are spiritual gifts."[3] The same is true for those who desire full-time vocational ministry. If, after taking steps one through four, you believe God has given you the gift of evangelism or teaching, then you need to share your faith or involve yourself in a teaching ministry. While the experience could prove awkward initially, given a little time, you will know whether or not you are gifted.

Clinton adds two other helpful insights. First, he writes, "Potential leaders are intuitively attracted to leaders who have the same spiritual gifts."[4] For example, you might feel a strong attraction to the preaching or teaching aspects of your pastor's ministry. Or you might feel attracted to a lay person who ministers with the gift of helps in a nearby hospital.

Second, Clinton writes, "Potential leaders respond intuitively to ministry challenges and assignments that call for their spiritual gift, even if not explicitly known."[5] For example, you might find yourself jumping at the opportunity to preach, lead a ministry, administer a project, or encourage a group of Christians.

Fulfillment

The next step after experience is fulfillment. As you focus on specific gifts and minister and experiment with your gift-mix, there will be a sense of personal satisfaction and a feeling of significance. You believe that what you are doing counts for something special, that the body of Christ is better because of you and your gifts, that you would be missed should you cease to minister with your gifts.

Although the motivation for using our gifts is unselfish—their ultimate purpose is to glorify God (1 Cor. 6:20), and they are for the common good (1 Cor. 12:7), not for ourselves (1 Cor. 13:5)—this sense of fulfillment is an important by-product that encourages us in the exercise of our gifts.

Confirmation

A seventh step in the discovery process is the confirmation of your gifts. This comes from two sources: your abilities and other people. First, as you become involved in various ministries, over time your gifts and abilities will begin to surface. When you focus on them and use them, you should see improvement and a corresponding desire to develop them further. You will begin to realize that these are, indeed, God's special gifts for you and will look forward to their use.

Second, other people will confirm your giftedness. The advice and counsel of others is a characteristic of wisdom: "Plans fail for lack of counsel, but with many advisers they succeed" (Prov. 15:22). Wise counselors include people such as a pastor, spouse, family, friends, and those to whom you minister. Give full attention to those who speak the truth in love. You do not need someone who tells you what they think you want to hear, or someone who is caustic and always negative. You need the input and confirmation of those who care about you and have your best interests at heart.

Fruit

An eighth step in gift discovery is ministry fruit or results. You need to ask, When I exercise my gifts, is there any fruit? If the Holy Spirit is operating through your gift-mix, there will be fruit. If you have the gift of evangelism, people will come to faith, or you will equip people who bring others to faith (Eph. 4:11–12). If you have the gift of teaching, your hearers will grow in knowledge of Scripture and biblical insight, and they will apply it to their lives. Also, your class or small group will, under most circumstances, grow numerically. If you have the gift of leadership, then people will follow that leadership.

Discovering Your Passion

According to chapter 3, your passion is your God-given capacity to fervently attach yourself to an object over an extended period of time to meet a need. The following approach to the discovery of your passion is both objective and subjective.

The Objective Approach

Read the following questions carefully. Give yourself plenty of time to think about them and feel free to return to them periodically. Remember, the discovery process will take place over an extended period of time. You need not answer all the questions below, nor is there a right or wrong answer to each, but several of them should catalyze your thinking and the ultimate discovery of your passion.

1. Do you have a "burning conviction" that a certain ministry is the most important place that God would have you? If so, what is it?

2. Does your gift-mix or gift-cluster point in a particular vocational or nonvocational direction? For example, Billy Graham has obvious gifts in evangelism, preaching, and leadership. His primary gift is evangelism, which is supported by his other gifts. These have pointed him vocationally toward the leadership of an evangelistic ministry that involves preaching.

3. Do you have a "burning, gut-level desire" to reach a particular group of people, such as the lost, unchurched, undiscipled, unborn, poor, oppressed, youth, children, college age, adults, business people, street people, alcoholics, homosexuals, AIDS sufferers, internationals, refugees, a particular ethnic group, cults, unwed mothers, single parents, young couples, singles, divorced, street gangs, military people, apartment dwellers?

4. Do you have a strong desire to pursue a particular issue as your ministry? Do any of the following causes stir you emotionally: the family, abortion, physical and emotional abuse, emotional problems, divorce, drug abuse, alcoholism, civil rights, politics, women's rights, poverty, AIDS, starving children, legalism, the clarity of the gospel, demonism? This could include a particular issue or cause in your church or community.

5. Does the pursuit of a particular subject area excite you? Examples include apologetics, cults, theology, the law, business, leadership, politics, government, finances, the arts.

6. Do you find yourself strongly attracted to a particular geographical area for ministry, such as an urban, suburban, or rural area located in a specific city, county, state, or foreign country?

7. Do you have a significant attraction to a particular area of ministry in your church, such as leading a small group, teaching a class, ministering to a particular age group, maintaining the building and grounds?

8. If money, family, and time were not factors, what would you want to do for the rest of your life in your work, in your ministry, in your church?

9. Do you have a secret ambition, something you have always wanted to pursue but were afraid to tell anyone?

The Subjective Approach

Turn back to the section on passion in chapter 3. When you first read this section, did you get a sense of what your passion might be? Carefully reread the section focusing on the elements of passion: fervency, object, tenure, and need. In light of these elements, write down any initial thoughts regarding your passion.

Discovering Your Temperament

The identification of your temperament will help you deepen your understanding of yourself and others. A knowledge of temperament allows us to see more clearly the strengths and the liabilities we and others bring to ministry. The approach to discovering temperament will be both objective and subjective.

The objective approach involves taking a temperament inventory and should prove more valid than the subjective approach. The problem with the subjective approach is that intentionally or unintentionally you can influence the results. You may choose a temperament type that appeals or seems best to you but does not reflect who you are. The objective approach attempts to eliminate the subjective element by asking a series of random questions that surface your real temperament identity. I have provided two objective temperament inventories in the appendixes at the back of this book.[6] One is patterned after model 1 and is called Temperament Indicator 1. The other is patterned after model 2 and is called Temperament Indicator 2. Turn to Indicator 1 in appendix B and complete it before reading any further.

I recommend that in addition to these inventories you take either the Biblical Personal Profile or the Personal Profile. They have been carefully refined and are sophisticated instruments that will result in a far more accurate assessment of your temperament.[7] If you take one of the two profiles and your results differ from Indicator 1, then opt for the former in light of its validity.

Also helpful are several books that are based on the four-temperament model. In addition to taking one of the profiles, read Voges and Braund's *Understanding How Others Misunderstand You* and Phillips's *The Delicate Art of Dancing with Porcupines*.[8]

Now turn to Temperament Indicator 2 in appendix C and complete it before proceeding. In addition to Indicator 2, you should take the Myers-Briggs Temperament Inventory (MBTI).[9] Like the two inventories above, it is a reliable instrument and will go into much greater depth than Indicator 2. A shorter form of the MBTI and one that is easier to obtain is the Keirsey Temperament Sorter.[10] If you desire more information on both forms, purchase a copy of the book *Please Understand Me* by Keirsey and Bates from your local bookstore.[11] This book contains the Keirsey Temperament Sorter. If the result of either of these inventories differs from those of Indicator 2, opt for the MBTI or the KTS.

Once you have taken the MBTI or the Kiersey Temperament Sorter, several books may prove helpful. *Please Understand Me* gives further knowledge and insight into your temperament based on the MBTI. Another work that applies the MBTI material to professional ministry is *Personality Type and Religious Leadership* by Oswald and Kroeger.[12]

The subjective approach to discovering your temperament is an affinity approach that involves reading a general description of the temperaments and determining which best describes you.

Model 1

Model 1 (so named for the sake of discussion) uses the traditional four-temperament grid that goes back to Hippocrates and is a variation of the Personal or Biblical Personal Profile. Read through the following descriptions and determine as best you can whether you are primarily a doer, influencer, relator, or thinker.

Doers

Doers attempt to control or overcome their environment to accomplish their ministry vision or mission. They are more task-oriented than people-oriented. They are catalytic people who love a challenge and are not afraid to take risks. Doers make quick decisions and like immediate results. They prefer change, and love to challenge the status quo. In their ministry environment they need freedom from control and supervision and desire opportunities for individual accomplishments. They are "upfront" and "out-front" people. They are Ds on the Biblical Personal Profile, and a biblical example is Paul.[13]

Influencers

Influencers attempt to persuade people to accomplish the ministry's vision. They are more people-oriented than task-oriented. They are persuaders and promote their ideas to bring others into alliance with them. Influencers enjoy contact with people and desire to make a favorable impression. They are articulate, motivational, and enthusiastic. They, too, prefer change and will challenge the status quo. In their ministry environment they need freedom from control and detail to function at their maximum ministry effectiveness. They, like doers, are upfront and out-front people. They are usually an "I" on the Biblical Personal Profile, and a biblical example is Peter.[14]

Relators

Relators cooperate with others to accomplish their vision. They are more people-oriented than task-oriented, and prefer the status quo unless given good reasons to change. They are patient, loyal, and good listeners. They are well-liked and pleasant to be around. They minister best in a secure and somewhat safe environment where they receive credit and appreciation for their accomplishments. While they can serve out-front, they prefer remaining behind the scenes. They are Ss on the Biblical Personal Profile, and a biblical example is Abraham.[15]

Thinkers

Thinkers tend to be diplomatic with people and comply with authority. They shape their ministry environment by promoting high quality and accuracy in accomplishing the ministry's vision and mission. Thinkers are more task-oriented than people-oriented. They are analytical and critical thinkers who focus on key details and accuracy. In their ministry environment, they desire to work under known circumstances and prefer the status quo. Like relators, they too can minister out-front, particularly as teachers and preachers, but often they prefer to minister behind the scenes, especially in terms of leadership. They are often Cs on the Biblical Personal Profile, and an example is Moses.

Model 2

The second model is that of the Myers-Briggs Temperament Inventory (MBTI). This model assumes that people approach four key areas of life in ways that are different but equally correct. These areas are called preferences because each person prefers one over the other much as we prefer to throw a ball with either our right or left hand. Carefully read through the following descriptions and determine which most accurately describes your preferences.

Extraverts/Introverts

The first area looks at where people like to focus their attention and interests and what is their source of emotional energy.

Extraverts like to work with the outer world of people and things. They prefer variety and action. They are energized by contact with large numbers of people and are good at greeting people. When they are by themselves for long periods of time, they become fatigued and seek out people who stimulate and revitalize them. Consequently they have many friends and acquaintances. They usually communicate freely and often act quickly, sometimes without thinking.

Introverts like the inner world of concepts and ideas. They prefer to spend time alone reading, studying, or meditating, and are emotionally drained if around many people for a long time. When fatigued, they are revitalized by "getting away from it all." They often have trouble remembering names and faces. Consequently they have a limited number of acquaintances and only a few close friends. They are careful with details and like to work on projects for long periods of time without interruption.

Sensing/Intuition

The second area looks at how people take in and process information.

Sensing people prefer to take in information through their senses. They focus on facts and details that can be observed through the five senses—what they can see, hear, touch, taste, or smell. They are practical people who prefer to do ministry rather than study ministry, and they like to follow established, traditional ways. They are steady workers who love to follow systems and procedures and to reach conclusions one step at a time. They dwell on present reality (the here-and-now), so for them "seeing is believing." An example in the Bible is Thomas, who needed to see and touch the Savior to believe (John 20:24–25).

Intuitive people take in information holistically, preferring the world of ideas, possibilities, and relationships. They are big-picture types who shy away from meticulous facts and figures. They like to solve problems and work in bursts of energy powered by enthusiasm. They do not care for systems and procedures but would rather pursue change and new ideas. Intuitive types prefer to follow their inspirations whether good or bad. They are visionary people who focus on the possible future (what could be). For them "believing is seeing." A biblical example is Nehemiah, who could see the rebuilt walls of Jerusalem before they had been rebuilt.

Thinking/Feeling

The third area concerns what you do with the information you take in, or how you make decisions.

Thinking people make their decisions on the basis of logic and objective analysis and are relatively unemotional. They prefer to win people over by their logic. They take a more impersonal approach to decision making in ministry and can come across at times as insensitive and not interested in people's feelings. The truth is important to them, and they are task-oriented. They are not people-pleasers and can minister in a team environment where there is some disharmony among the ministry team.

Feeling people make their decisions on the basis of personal values and motives. They are aware of other people and their feelings. They prefer to win people over through persuasion. Feeling types take a personal approach to decision making and communicate warmth and harmony. Human values are important; consequently they are more people-oriented. They can be people-pleasers and prefer a ministry environment where there is harmony among the ministry team.

Judging/Perceiving

The last area deals with how you orient to the outer world and to structure and the time it takes to make decisions.

Judging people prefer a more structured approach to life because they desire to control and regulate life. Thus they are organized and deal with the world in a planned and orderly way. They minister at their best when they can plan their work and follow that plan without change and interruption. They may not see new things that need to be done, however. Preferring to have things settled and behind them, they pursue closure and tend to make decisions quickly.

Perceiving people seek to understand life and adapt to it, and so they take a less structured approach to life. They are adaptable, flexible, and spontaneous. They tend to start too many projects and have difficulty finishing what they start. Perceiving people are curious about and enjoy exploring new ideas and ministries. They have little need for closure and prefer to make decisions only after all the facts are in.

Discovering Your Leadership Role and Style

Leadership is critical to the success of any work for Christ. As the leadership of a ministry goes, so goes the ministry itself. Two important leadership areas are your leadership role and style.

Your Leadership Role

There are two primary leadership roles, leadership and management or administration. Most likely you are some combination of both, but one role will dominate. Discovering your leadership role involves first an objective and then a subjective approach.

The Objective Approach

To help you discover your leadership role I have designed a tool called the Leadership Role Indicator.[16] Turn to the Leadership Role Indicator in appendix D. Complete and score it.

The Subjective Approach

Turn back to the section on leadership role in chapter 3. As you read through this section, did you identify with or feel an attraction toward leadership or management? Carefully reread this section paying particular attention to the descriptions given for both leaders and managers. Note the definitions, differences, and the possibility that you may be a combination of both leader and manager. If the latter, which is stronger—leadership or management?

Your Leadership Style

While everyone may not have the gift of leadership, I believe everyone has to some degree the natural, God-given ability to lead. Your style of leadership reflects how you lead people. Your style may be determined both objectively and subjectively.

The Objective Approach

To take the objective approach, you need to have completed Temperament Indicator 1 or the Biblical Personal Profile or the Personal Profile. As noted in chapter 3, if you are a D, your leadership style is autocratic; if you are an I, it is democratic; if you are an R or S, it is participatory; and if you are a T or C, it is bureaucratic. Remember, you are the final judge on these matters. If this assessment does not ring true, then retake the instruments or wait a few months and retake them. It is possible that they did not accurately reflect your leadership style.

Most likely you will be a combination of two of the four temperaments in the Biblical Personal Profile or the Personal Profile. One will be primary and the other secondary, and your resulting leadership style will reflect characteristics of both. For instance your style may be primarily democratic (if you are high I) and also autocratic (if you are a secondary D).

The Subjective Approach

Turn back to the section on leadership styles in chapter 3. When you first read through this section, did you identify with or feel an attraction toward the autocratic, democratic, participatory, or bureaucratic style? Carefully reread this section paying particular attention to the descriptions given to all four styles. Note the definitions, differences, and the distinct possibility that you may be a combination of two styles.

Discovering Your Evangelism Style

Little has been written regarding the Christian's style of evangelism. Therefore this approach to discovering your style or combination of styles is more subjective than objective.

The Objective Approach

A clue to your evangelism style is how you relate to people in general. Therefore one of the more objective temperament inventories, such as Temperament Indicator 1, the Biblical Personal Profile, or the Personal Profile, can give you insight into how you prefer to evangelize.

First, I have observed a correlation between a high D temperament and a confrontational evangelistic style. Those who use a confrontational style experience a lot of rejection: doors slammed in their faces, people rudely saying they are not interested. While all the temperaments struggle with rejection, Ds tend to handle it best. I also see some correlation with the testimonial style. Those who use it deal primarily with the facts. For example, the blind man healed in John 9 kept responding to his questioners, "One thing I do know. I was blind but now I see!" (v. 25). High Ds also place great value on facts.

Second, I have noted a correlation between high I and R or S temperaments and the relational and invitational styles. Both high "I"s and Rs or Ss are people-oriented temperaments, and the relational and invitational styles involve time and interaction with people. They focus on winning family and friends to Christ. In Mark 5, Jesus told the man delivered from demon-possession to "Go home to your family and tell them how much the Lord has done for you, and how he has had mercy on you" (v. 19). In John 4, the Samaritan woman went back to her people and said, "Come, see a man who told me everything I ever did. Could this be the Christ?" (v. 29).

Third, I have observed a correlation between the high T or C temperaments and the intellectual style. Those who use the intellectual style tend to be extremely intelligent, analytical, and able to put together good arguments for their belief systems. They enjoy grappling with the tough questions of Christianity. People with the high T or C temperaments are also analytical and intelligent.

Each temperament will have strengths and weaknesses in evangelism. A high D temperament with the gift of evangelism will be a self-starter who will see many come to faith in Christ. This person may be seen as overbearing and pushy, however. A high I temperament gifted in evangelism will be an enthusiastic, articulate witness who relates well with unbelievers and wins many to Christ. However, they tend to worry too much about what others think about them. The high S temperament with the evangelistic gift will be a steady, faithful witness for Christ who gets along extremely well with non-Christians. However, they tend to be easily intimidated and will not take risks like the high D or the high I. Finally, the high C temperament with the gift of evangelism is careful in witnessing to the lost. They are analytical and concerned with details. It is important to them to have the correct answers for any questions an unbeliever might ask. However, they can be too cautious and inflexible.[17]

The Subjective Approach

To determine your style subjectively, reread the section on evangelism styles in chapter 3, and think about your past activity in evangelism, which should give you some idea as to what works for you and what does not.

If you have had any evangelism experience, for example, most likely you have been exposed to the confrontational style. You may have knocked on people's doors, gone witnessing in a college dorm, or handed out tracts on a street corner. You are either attracted to this style or repelled by it.

You need to expose yourself to other styles as well. Your church may be a good place to start. If your church doesn't offer opportunities for evangelism, I have two suggestions. First, look for people in your church who are individually sharing their faith. Most likely, they would be delighted to help and involve you in some form of evangelism. Second, contact a parachurch ministry in your area that specializes in evangelism. Most are looking for workers and would be willing to help you. However, be aware that some churches and parachurch ministries specialize in only one style of evangelism: confrontational.

Discovering Your Natural Gifts and Talents

No doubt you have always been more aware of your natural God-given gifts and talents than your other design components. Since they were inborn, you have lived with them longer than your spiritual gifts. Also, the world around you focuses more on these abilities and their discovery than some of the other areas of your design, so they are more familiar and recognizable.

The Objective Approach

Turn to the Natural Gifts and Talents Inventory in appendix E and complete the inventory before you proceed.

If you plan to pursue full-time vocational ministry, you may need to consider additional part-time opportunities outside of the church and parachurch. This applies to pastoral ministry in particular. Presently the supply of pastors is larger than the demand. Also, the majority of churches in North America are small. Pastors often need additional employment ("tent-making") to supplement their salaries. Consequently I have provided a Natural Gifts and Abilities Indicator in appendix F. If you do not anticipate vocational ministry, this indicator can help you further identify your natural abilities for your present or future vocation.

Various individuals and organizations have developed a number of tools to help people discover their unique, motivated abilities or have set up organizations to help with the same. One helpful vocational tool is the Campbell Interest and Skills Survey.[18] In addition, you might want to contact a vocational counselor or vocational testing service in your community, which are located at some public high schools, community colleges, and universities.

The Subjective Approach

Depending on your age, you have already determined many of your natural abilities. For example, you may have taken piano or voice lessons beginning at an early age and have determined your abilities to play an instrument or sing. However, you have other abilities that you have not discovered or are vaguely aware of. To continue the process of bringing them to the surface, reread the section on natural gifts and talents in chapter 3, especially the part on the essence of natural gifts.

A helpful tool in discovering and confirming your natural abilities and the other components of your design is the "life map" or "life line," which is a pictorial representation of your life from birth to present. A careful examination of the past serves to bring to light patterns of consistent behavior that, in turn, reveal our giftedness and various styles through which we operate. To develop your life map, trace your life from as far back as you can remember up to today, searching for clues and hints that help you to discover your spiritual gifts, passion, and temperament. Look for important accomplishments, hobbies, jobs, interests, and trends that reveal natural abilities and other design elements.

The life map often surfaces design features that you may not have been aware of. You might discover that you have always been motivated to start new things. For example, in grade school you may have organized a lawn-

Life Map

Time Line

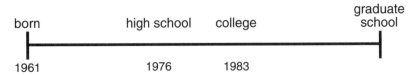

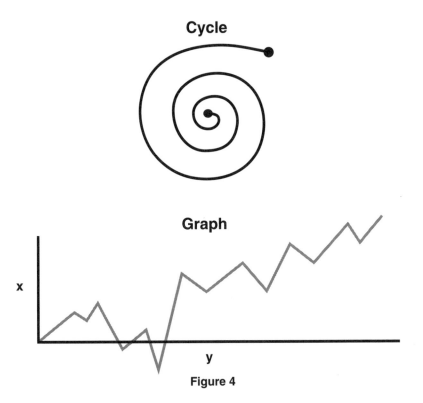

mowing business in the summer to earn a few extra dollars. Then in high school you started a documents-delivery service. Later in life you started another business, not to mention a neighborhood Bible study. This pattern demonstrates that a significant part of your design is starting new ministries, whether as a lay or professional person in a church or parachurch ministry.

In *The Leadership Challenge*, Kouzes and Posner present a helpful, abbreviated version of a lifeline exercise developed by Shepard and Hawley.[19]

On a blank piece of paper, draw your "lifeline." Start as far back as you can remember and stop at the present time.

Draw your lifeline as a graph, with the peaks representing the highs in your life and the valleys representing the lows.

Next to each peak, write a word or two identifying the peak experience. Do the same for the valleys.

Now go back over each peak. For each peak, make a few notes on why this was a peak experience for you.

Analyze your notes. What themes and patterns are revealed by the peaks in your life? What important personal strengths are revealed? What do these themes and patterns tell you about what you are likely to find personally compelling in the future?[20]

The life map can take several forms. Kouzes and Posner suggest a graph. However, you may find another figure is more to your style. Some people have used a straight timeline, a corkscrew spiraling from the inside out, or a picture (see figure 4). Whatever form you use, the composition of your life map is critical ultimately to discovering and understanding your divine design. It will open your eyes to how God has wondrously designed you (Ps. 139:14) and will motivate you to use your design in his service. Before you proceed with the exercise at the end of this chapter, be sure to compose your life map according to the guidelines above.

Worksheet

To see a complete picture of how God has designed you, place all the information you have gleaned from this chapter under the appropriate topic.

1. What are your spiritual gifts? Is one a primary gift around which the others cluster in support? If so, list it first and circle it.

a.

b.

    c.

    d.

    e.

2. What is your passion?

3. What is your temperament? (Circle the appropriate letters.)

    a. Temperament Indicator 1: DIRT
    b. The Biblical or Personal Profile: DiSC
    c. Temperament Indicator 2

$$
\begin{array}{ll}
\text{E} & \text{I} \\
\text{S} & \text{N} \\
\text{T} & \text{F} \\
\text{J} & \text{P}
\end{array}
$$

    d. The Myers-Briggs Temperament Inventory

$$
\begin{array}{ll}
\text{E} & \text{I} \\
\text{S} & \text{N} \\
\text{T} & \text{F} \\
\text{J} & \text{P}
\end{array}
$$

4. What is your leadership role?

    a. Leader
    b. Manager
    c. Leader-manager
    d. Manager-leader

5. What is your leadership style? If you express two styles, circle both and underline the one that is dominant.

   a. Autocratic
   b. Democratic
   c. Participatory
   d. Bureaucratic

6. What is your evangelistic style(s)?

7. What are your natural gifts and talents?

8. Optional: What is your style of spiritual growth, learning, conflict resolution, thinking, and teamwork?

9. List any other relevant observations about your divine design.

Part 2

Determining Your
Personal Vision
for Ministry

The second part of this book will help you understand that God has a limited range of ministries for you in the body of Christ. Once you have discovered your ministry identity (part 1), the next step is to use this information to determine what ministry God has for you—which is the ultimate goal of this book (part 2).

The Concept of
Personal Vision

5

Is Every Member a Minister?

Carol sat down with a cup of steaming black coffee and the day's mail, feeling puzzled and a little troubled. The church's lay-ministries consultant, Bruce Smith, had mailed the results of her spiritual gifts inventory. No explanation accompanied the results, just a note saying, "drop by and see me at your convenience so we can talk about your results and your ministry vision."

The inventory said God had given her the spiritual gifts of leadership, mercy, and pastor. The first two she understood. However, she had some concern over the gift of pastor—what did that mean? She did not believe women should pastor churches, and she thought you had to be "called" to be a pastor. She had never had a deep, emotional experience like her pastor back home in south Texas, where God speaks in a vision and calls a person to go into the ministry and pastor a church. Isn't that what a "ministry vision" is?

Lately Carol's new pastor had said that a major goal for the people in this new paradigm church is "Every member a minister." But what does that mean? She was perfectly happy as an attorney—was God telling her to change professions? *First thing tomorrow,* she thought, *I'll call and make an appointment with Bruce Smith.*

Once you have discerned how God has wired you for ministry (your divine design or ministry identity), the next step is to discover your ministry vision (your design-based direction). Now that you have some knowledge of who you are, you need to discover what you can do. But before you attempt this, we must answer several questions. First, who is to be involved in ministry? Can every member be a minister? Should everyone in church pursue vocational ministry? Second, what is a ministry vision? Is it an emotional experience in which God speaks to you in a dream and tells you what to do? Finally, we will look at several issues that swirl around the concept of ministry vision, such as, Does a person have to experience a divine call to be involved in ministry?

Who Is Involved in Ministry?

So far this book has assumed that every Christian is to be involved in some form of ministry whether full- or part-time. But does the Bible teach this, and are most believers involved to some degree in ministry?

The Plan for Ministry Mobilization

Is every member a minister? Yes! God desires that all who know the Savior be involved in ministry to some degree. Our loving Father's plan is to bless us and others through our involvement in serving him and the church. God does not recognize the lay-clergy division that has characterized the church for so many thousands of years. Clergy are not paid to do the work of the ministry in our place. This is evident from God's many divine accomplishments in our lives.

First, God created each of us with a unique design (Gen. 1:26–28; 2:15; Exod. 31:1–5; Ps. 119:73; 139:13–16; Jer. 1:5; Luke 1:15; Gal. 1:15). This includes our temperament and natural talents and gifts.

Second, God has given the Holy Spirit to each of us. At the moment of our conversion to Christ, God, the Holy Spirit, indwells each of us (1 Cor. 3:16; 6:19), supplying us with the power we need to accomplish our ministry vision in this world (Eph. 3:16, 20).

Third, Christ has placed each of us in a unique relationship in a community of believers called the body of Christ (1 Cor. 12). In this context, he has also given each of us one or more spiritual gifts, which are an addition to our design when we come to faith in him (Eph. 4:7–11).

Fourth, we are all believer-priests due to our position in Christ (1 Peter 2:5–9; Rev. 1:6). Our priesthood involves sacrifice, worship, and prayer. Sacrificial service includes our commitment to God as well as our praise and giving. Worship includes acts of adoration, confession, and thanksgiving. Finally, prayer includes intercession for God's people and ourselves as we accomplish his work.

Fifth, the Father has placed all of us in various difficult situations in life for more effective service (2 Cor. 1:3–7). No one will experience all of life's difficulties. Instead God allows different Christians to go through trials and tragedies and then uses them to minister to others in similar situations. For example, a mother who has experienced the death of a child can have a significant ministry in the lives of other mothers who have lost children.

We are never more like Christ than when we serve him, and these divine accomplishments enable us to minister his grace in the lives of believers and unbelievers alike. God desires more from us than merely showing up on Sunday and filling a pew.

The Problem of Ministry Mobilization

Far too many Christians are not involved in any ministry, while others are not properly involved, having been placed in positions contrary to their designs.

Larry Richards and his colleagues quizzed 5,000 pastors about the greatest needs in their churches. From a list of twenty-five items, nearly 100 percent of the pastors selected as the top or second priority "Getting my lay people involved as ministering men and women."[1] This is why Carol's pastor developed the slogan "Every Member a Minister." He is not suggesting that the entire congregation give up their current professions and pursue vocational ministry as pastors. His desire is to mobilize them for ministry in the body of Christ (Eph. 4:11–12).

There are several reasons for inactivity and wrong activity. One is the typical North American church service that takes place on Sunday morning, particularly in churches that place an emphasis on teaching over worship. Teaching is a necessary but passive function that can encourage passivity on the part of Christians. The pastor or teacher does all the work while the congregation sits and listens. In most churches this is the main event for the entire week; everything else pales in significance.

A second reason is the way some churches recruit people for ministry. The process is based on emotion or coercion. The pastor or a well-meaning Sunday school superintendent plays on the emotions of members until they agree to serve. They may pester members or preach "serve or burn" sermons until members finally give in and agree to take that class of dysfunctional fifth graders.

A third reason for the "unemployment" rolls is the lack of knowledge and expertise of pastors doing the recruiting. They simply do not know what they are doing. Their seminary or Bible college never offered a course on lay mobilization.

A fourth reason why lay people often do not respond is they are waiting for a personal invitation. Many churches make an announcement regarding the church's needs and then sit back and wait for people to respond. Some people do, but many do not. I have discovered in ministry that people respond more to a personal, private invitation. They are not opposed to involvement; they simply want someone to come and ask for it.

A fifth reason is some pastors do not recognize or value the ministry of lay people. Their attitude may be "If you want it done well, then you have to do it yourself." Some feel that since they have been to seminary, they are responsible to do the work of the ministry; after all, that is their job. Others attempt to minister out of codependency. They do all the ministry because they feel good when others need them.

A sixth reason behind lay inactivity is many lay people are convinced that ministry is the pastor's responsibility. This is a reversal of reason five. This is the attitude of the people in Carol's church in south Texas. Since the pastor has been to school or in ministry for a long time, he is responsible to do the work of the ministry. Their job is to be faithful and committed, which means showing up on Sunday morning and putting their tithe in the offering plate.

The discovery of your divine design and personal ministry direction is one major solution to these problems. God wants all believers involved in ministry because that is what is best for them and the body of Christ. The proper discovery of your design and direction will motivate you not only toward involvement but the right kind of ministry involvement.

What Is a Ministry Vision?

It is one thing to realize and accept that God desires the involvement of all Christians in ministry. It is another to understand what that involvement entails. Developing your ministry vision can give you that understanding. But what is a ministry vision?

Personal Ministry Vision

A personal ministry vision resembles an organizational ministry vision. Both concern people. One difference between them, however, is that organizational vision affects all the people who make up that organization; whereas personal vision primarily affects the individual alone. In my book *Vision America*, I discuss organizational vision.[2] It is not to be confused with the ministry organization's purpose or philosophy. The same is true for personal ministry vision.

Purpose

Just as a ministry organization has a purpose for its existence, so does each individual Christian. The purpose of both is to glorify God, just as the purpose of the nation of Israel was to glorify God (Ps. 22:23; 50:15; Isa. 24:15). The Hebrew term for this idea means to honor or value someone who is worthy of respect and obedience. To honor or value them is to enhance their reputation privately or publicly. In the New Testament as well, the church's purpose is to glorify God (Rom. 15:9; 2 Cor. 9:13). The New Testament term also means to honor or value someone and is literally translated "honor" in 1 Corinthians 6:20. Consequently, the people of God are here on earth to value and honor God in their lives, enhancing his excellent reputation before a watching world.

That is our proper purpose in life—it is why we exist. It is the key to the meaning of our entire existence. It is the thread that runs through the history of each of us, connecting all its events and relationships, giving true meaning to our lives. Without it life becomes superficial, empty, and meaningless (read Ecclesiastes!). While each event and each person in our lives has a unique purpose, they all are subsumed under a greater purpose: God's glory. To miss that greater purpose is to miss life altogether, because all of life is centered in God, not us (Col. 1:15–20; Heb. 1:1–4). Unfortunately this is difficult to see and realize from our limited view of life.

In Acts 13:36, Paul summarizes David's entire life with the words: "For when David had served God's purpose in his own generation, he fell asleep; he was buried with his fathers and his body decayed." David's life served God's purpose. Most of what he did (certainly not all) brought honor to God and enhanced God's great reputation before others. That is why David existed.

Understanding your life's purpose is critical to discovering your life's vision. It assumes you understand why you exist. However, your ministry vision is not to be confused with your purpose. Instead your ministry vision serves to accomplish your purpose—God's glory. Ministry vision is not the same as purpose but is subsumed under that purpose.

Philosophy of Ministry

Individual Christians and ministry organizations have a philosophy of ministry. An organization's philosophy of ministry is its core values. The ministry's core values determine its priorities and shape all its ministry decisions. The philosophy of ministry also answers the *why* question—why does the ministry organization do what it does? Lyle Schaller writes, "The most important single element of any corporate, congregational, or denominational culture, however, is the value system. . . . The values of any organization control priorities, provide the foundation for formulating goals, and set the tone and direction for the organization."[3] One core value might be that people matter to God. If this is a value, then much of what a ministry does will reflect a caring, loving attitude toward all people.

Each believer's philosophy of ministry consists of his or her core values. What you value in ministry will shape and direct all that you do or do not do in ministry. Your philosophy of ministry controls your ministry priorities, formulates your goals, and sets the tone for the direction of your ministry. One core value might be your attitude toward Scripture. Do you believe that the Bible is God's inspired and trustworthy rule of faith and practice for all Christians? Another might be your attitude toward prayer, or your feelings about change. Do you have a commitment to prayer and an appreciation for innovation in ministry?

Your ministry vision is not the same as your core ministry values. Your ministry vision rises out of your core values. If a core ministry value is that lost people matter to God, then your personal ministry vision will focus to a great degree on reaching lost people.

Ministry Direction

Your ministry vision is the same as your ministry direction (design-based direction) or in more contemporary terms your "ministry niche" or "ministry portfolio." It is where you fit in the body of Christ. It is your specific ministry or range of ministries—what you can do in serving the Savior.

Believers, like ministry organizations, have a mission in life. The mission of the church is the Great Commission (Matt. 28:19–20; Mark 16:15) which in turn serves our greater purpose: to glorify God. The mission of each Christian is their particular place in the accomplishment of the Great Commission.

Therefore I could use the terms *ministry vision* or *ministry mission*. There are some similarities and distinctions between the two. Both answer the *what* question: What is my ministry in obedience to the Great Commission? However, your personal ministry mission is more goal-oriented. It is a short, straightforward, "nuts and bolts" statement of what you do, as might be found in a job description: I am a Sunday school teacher, a small-group leader, a teacher of adults, a greeter, a senior pastor, a worship director.

However, your personal ministry vision articulates what that ministry looks like as you see it in your head or attempt to communicate it to others. It is what you see when you think about your mission. It is usually longer and contains more imagery than the mission statement. Rather than the kind of thing you would read in a job description, it is what you might see in a promotional brochure. For example, a person who goes into vocational ministry as a church planter might have the following ministry mission: "My mission is to plant Great Commission churches that plant other churches throughout Dallas, Texas." Whereas a ministry vision might be "My ministry vision is to birth significant Great Commission churches throughout the city of Dallas that will see unchurched, lost people embrace the Savior and hurting families healed and brought back together in Christ. These in turn will plant other reproducing churches with the result that in fifteen years Christian influence will be increasingly felt all over the metroplex, the state of Texas, and abroad."

A ministry mission for a lay person might be "I teach a class of junior high boys at our church." It could be expanded into the following vision statement: "I spend several hours each week providing spiritual insight and wisdom from Scripture for a group of young men who are at a critical time of development in their personal lives." The vision is the mission statement fleshed out in imaginative, descriptive terms of the community and the people who live in it.

The distinction between a personal mission and vision may only be slight; however, there is a difference. In some cases, that difference is how the statement affects the listener. What might be a mission statement for one could be a vision statement for another if it elicits a strong mental picture of what the ministry will look like. Consequently the terms *vision* and *mission* may be used synonymously in this book along with other terms such as *ministry direction, ministry niche, ministry job, ministry portfolio.*

Regardless, you should take time out of your busy schedule to begin writing your personal ministry vision. The process should begin as you finish this chapter and flourish by the end of chapter 6. This is a very important part of the formation of your vision or mission statement. I suggest that you set aside a morning or two each week for this process or, better still, spend a day or two at the beach. The format is not important. Perhaps one that I have used above might prove helpful.

Ministry Vision Issues

Much of Carol's confusion in the introduction to this chapter stems from various issues that have collected like barnacles to the concept of Christian ministry. Some of the issues that affect the concept of ministry vision are calling versus design, old versus new paradigms, church versus parachurch, and gifts versus office.

Ministry Calling Versus Ministry Design

The concept of the calling of God is widely used by many as an indispensable factor in determining God's will for the believer's life in general and the believer's pursuit of a vocation in particular. Pastor Kent Hughes writes, "My call to ministry was *real!* And I am convinced that God calls certain of his children to this special service. To be sure, my experience of the call is not normative for anyone else, for the experience of God's call is as varied as there are people; only the reality is the same."[4]

In this view, professional ministry is a higher calling for Christians than professions such as law or banking. In fact, it is the "highest of calls." Hughes quotes Dr. Will Houghton, a former pastor: "The highest calling man can know is the call to the Christian ministry. While it is true that every Christian is commissioned to labor together with Christ, it is also true that he has chosen some to undertake special service for him in their day and generation."[5]

In this view, God issues a special, higher call for a lifetime of vocational ministry to certain individuals whom he has chosen. Again, God is active in choosing, while man passively receives. Most often the call is to the vocational ministry of a pastor or missionary. God accomplishes this call in a variety of ways, most of which are described as a subjective "inner call." For example, the Holy Spirit may call men through a special inner conviction, an unusual urge to preach the gospel, or by impressing a particular passage of Scripture on one's mind.

Regardless of what constitutes a special call to vocational ministry or how that is accomplished, the real issue is whether or not the concept is scriptural. Hughes believes it is. He writes, "Those who would deny or minimize the fact that God calls individual Christians to special service must not only discount the facts of human experience but the evidence of Scripture, which records the calls of Moses, Isaiah, Jeremiah, Paul, and the commissioning of the apostles."[6] The classic text in support of this idea is Isaiah 6:1–13, where God calls Isaiah the prophet. Hughes believes this particular call has all the classic elements common to the experience of those who have obeyed God's call to minister: a vision of God's holiness, a vision of our unholiness, the forgiveness of sin, and obedience.[7]

However, further examination of the Bible indicates the concept of a special, divine call is not scriptural nor is it normative for all believers, for several reasons. First, to argue for this concept on subjective grounds alone raises problems and questions that most who hold this view will acknowledge. Its validity must rest on scriptural evidence. To argue for a special inner call, those who embrace the concept must demonstrate that the experiences of Moses, Isaiah, Jeremiah, and Paul are normative experiences for all who pursue vocational ministry in all ages. That these Old Testament prophets and some apostles had a special call from God does not necessarily mean others must as well. This argument is a non sequitur.

Also, these were prophets who spoke God's word and prophesied future events (Isa. 1:1; 7:14; 9:6; Jer. 1:7–9). Paul was an apostle with apostolic authority to record divine revelation. Neither Old Testament prophets nor New Testament apostles are the equivalent of the contemporary pastoral office.

Second, the offices or positions of elders and deacons in the New Testament are the closest equivalent to today's office of pastor. In light of the significant size of the early, first-century churches, the elders spent a lot of time with their ministries and were compensated for them (1 Tim. 5:17–18; 1 Peter 5:2). Much of that ministry involved shepherding God's flock (Acts 20:28; 1 Peter 5:1–2) as well as preaching to and teaching God's people (1 Tim. 5:17). Of the fifteen or more qualifications for elders and deacons listed in 1 Timothy 3:1–13 and Titus 1:5–9, a special inner call is not mentioned. Also 1 Timothy 3:1 indicates that people can "desire" or set their heart on being an elder. This clearly teaches personal proactivity on the part of the believer and contradicts the idea that God is active in the divine call while man remains passive.

Third, the New Testament uses the term for *call* or a form thereof more than 150 times. However, the term is primarily used of the divine call to salvation, never to vocational Christian ministry.

Fourth, in the analogy that the New Testament makes between the church and the human body (1 Cor. 12), no body part is separated out for special or separate ministry. While mention is made of the head, there is no indication that it was a special or divinely "called" body part.

Fifth, the New Testament teaches the priesthood of all believers (1 Peter 2:9–10; Rev. 1:6). There is no mention of a special priestly caste or a hierarchy of the few who are set aside for pastoral or missionary service.

The conclusion of this brief study is the same one reached earlier in this chapter—all believers are to be involved in ministry. The key to the exact nature of that ministry is not some special inner call from God but a person's divine design. Therefore men who desire the pastoral office in particular do not need to wait for a call to that office but need to determine if their design best suits them for the position. This pastoral design often consists of such gifts as leadership, administration, teaching, pastor.

Old Paradigms Versus New Paradigms

A relatively new term in literature on leadership, change, and ministry is *paradigm*. A paradigm is a shared set of assumptions and beliefs, a mindset or viewpoint about reality or how things are.[8]

Each ministry represents a paradigm. A church's paradigm is the particular assumptions, beliefs, or viewpoint about reality adopted and shared in common by the congregation. It includes not only the church's doctrinal beliefs, but what the congregation thinks about other areas of its life, such as the style of its music, where people sit in the service, what they wear to that service, if an invitation follows the service, how the offering is taken. In short "It's how we see and do things around here." Consequently the church's paradigm serves as a pair of glasses through which its people view the world and reality. It affects all they see and do.

No two churches have precisely the same paradigm. However, a number of churches share similar paradigms. A large number are referred to as traditional churches because they prefer church music that favors the grand old hymns of the faith played on an organ; the sermons may last forty-five minutes to an hour and may be preached from a particular translation of the Bible; the men wear coats and ties, and the women dresses; and there is a Sunday morning and evening service with a Wednesday evening prayer meeting. They are old paradigm churches because they see and do church the way it was done in North America back in the fifties and earlier.

Other churches view life through a different set of glasses. They prefer a style of music that is more upbeat and use instruments such as the guitar and drums. The worship consists of contemporary praise hymns that are printed on the bulletin or projected on screens placed at the front of the sanctuary, and the people dress casually as well as formally. The sermons are much shorter and attempt to be practical and relevant to the times. These are commonly referred to as contemporary or new paradigm churches. While new paradigm churches can be ministry restrictive (they have limited opportunities for lay ministries), most seem to offer a broader ministry menu than old paradigm churches. For example, few old paradigm churches include the fine arts as a part of worship or ministry (ballet, drama, painting, sculpture); as a result lost people naturally gifted in these areas are not attracted, nor do they find a place to exercise these gifts when they come to faith.[9]

In the past, paradigms have proved virile. Once in place they prevail over a ministry for years, decades, even centuries. However, with change occurring at lightning pace in the latter half of the twentieth century, paradigms are turning over more frequently. Consequently today's contemporary churches will soon become tomorrow's traditional paradigms, and new congregations with new paradigms will appear on the scene and be called contemporary churches.

Christians who serve in any capacity in a ministry must be aware of their paradigm preference. While some people in the different paradigms attempt to argue that their paradigm is the correct biblical paradigm corresponding to the first century church, no correct biblical paradigms exist. The real issue in most evangelical churches is not what is biblical and what is not—but which paradigm you prefer. An old paradigm church may not have a place of ministry for someone whose ministry vision is drama or leading a small group. A new paradigm church may not have a place of ministry for another whose ministry vision involves playing the organ or leading or singing in a choir. The issue in both examples is not which is biblical, since neither is forbidden in Scripture, but which you prefer. The same applies to those interested in vocational Christian ministry. Those who desire to pastor a church must be aware of their paradigm preference as well as the church's. The ministry world is full of horror stories of what happened to the young new pastor with a new paradigm mentality who tried to minister to a church with an old paradigm mentality.

Church Versus Parachurch

Should you attempt to minister in a church or a parachurch setting? Before going any further, I need to define these terms. The key to the term *parachurch* is the prefix "para," which means "along side of." *Parachurch* literally means "along side of the church." Here the term *church* refers to the local church and not the universal body of Christ (the fellowship of all believers).

In the last decade, some have begun to use the term *para-local church* instead of *parachurch*. In this book, I use the terms *parachurch* or *para-local church* of any ministry other than that of a local church. This would include such ministries as some missions organizations; Christian colleges, universities, and seminaries; youth ministries; ministries to children; ministries to international students; ministries to college students; ministries to cults; ministries to military personnel; ministries to athletes; ministries to ethnic groups; evangelistic ministries; counseling ministries; and publishing ministries.

Some trace the beginnings of the parachurch movement back to the Pietists in 1669, though the causes that promoted these movements were evident before then.[10] The movement has experienced its greatest expansion since 1860 and in the twentieth century in particular.[11] Leith Anderson writes that a large number of parachurch organizations were born and blossomed with the post-World War II "baby boom."[12] However, he believes that at the end of the 1980s many of these parachurch groups have reached their zenith: "But like the baby boomers, these organizations are starting to show signs of aging. Many of the founders are gone; many will go within the next decade or two. And the current generation of leaders, who often seem to lack the vision of the founders, are accused of merely managing others' dreams."[13] Still, I suspect and hope that the parachurch movement will continue to minister effectively in this world until the Savior returns.

In deciding where to pursue your ministry vision, the local church or parachurch, you might find it helpful to consider the advantages and disadvantages of both.

There are numerous advantages to ministry in the local church. Most churches, especially the large ones, offer a number of diverse ministry opportunities, which provide you with more opportunities to minister and be ministered to. Another advantage is ministry accountability. Even if a believer joins a parachurch ministry, all believers should be part of a local church, which has the greatest potential for ministering to and holding a broad number of Christians accountable for their lives and service. A third advantage is that churches often minister to a broad range of people. While people are attracted to a particular church on the basis of some affinity, most churches, especially larger churches, reflect some variety of people along racial, educational, social, and economic lines. A fourth advantage is consistent theology. Most churches have a doctrinal statement of their beliefs that is embraced by its members. A fifth advantage is most churches observe some form of the ordinances. Jesus Christ commanded believers to be baptized and partake of the elements of the Lord's Supper. The local church offers these to its people.

There are some disadvantages to ministry in the church. First, some churches focus on their buildings and not their people. Much time, money, and energy can go into bricks and mortar rather than people. Second, a tendency exists in some churches to place all their ministries in the hands of a few professionals. This creates an overworked clergy and a passive, lethargic laity. Third, most churches are slow to change. They are locked into old paradigm ministries that tend to be ministry restrictive. Fourth, far too many North American churches are having little if any evangelistic impact, especially in the unchurched community.

In *The Church and the Parachurch*, Jerry White lists several advantages to parachurch ministry. First, independent mission agencies have primarily been responsible for developing and initiating missions ministries over the last two centuries. Second, since lay people are at the core of most parachurch ministries, these ministries have done a good job of equipping and involving them in ministry. Third, parachurch organizations have done a good job of equipping and involving women, both single and married. Fourth, parachurch ministries have become experts in how to penetrate and evangelize the unique groups that make up our culture. Fifth, many of the finest educational institutions from elementary through graduate school are parachurch ministries. Sixth, parachurch ministries appear open to change and innovation, realizing that it takes all kinds of ministries to reach all kinds of people.[14]

White also lists several disadvantages. First, with some organizations no accountability exists except to the organization itself. Second, parachurch organizations often do not relate well to or support the local church. Third, because parachurch organizations are independent, there is needless duplication of some ministries and a lack of coordination with others. Fourth, most organizations begin with and often focus on one person whose vision and drive carries the ministry. This can result in obsessive control and the potential for a personality cult. Fifth, parachurch ministries are specialized, focusing only on part of believers' needs, not their total needs. Thus a special focus may be blown out of proportion, whereas other areas are missed entirely.[15]

Gifts Versus Office

A final issue that affects the implementation of your ministry vision—in a church in particular—is the difference between ministry gifts and church offices.

Every church consists of a body of Christians who have a cluster of spiritual gifts (1 Cor. 12; Rom. 12). Therefore the ministry of the church is the responsibility of all the people in the church. The corporate ministry of any church will only be as effective as the individual ministries of the believers in that church.

Every church will also have officers. Most argue that according to the Bible only two offices exist: elder (1 Tim. 3:1–13) and deacon (1 Tim. 3:8–13). Some would include women in the office of deaconess (1 Tim. 3:11) and point to Phoebe as an example (Rom. 16:1). One unique view identifies four offices in the church: Christ as the head (Col. 1:18; Eph. 1:22), elders (1 Tim. 3), deacons (1 Tim. 3), and priests (1 Peter 5:9). The latter includes all believers.[16]

With the exception of the last position, most agree that not all Christians in the church will hold an office though they are encouraged to seek the office of elder (1 Tim. 3:1). The offices, however, come with certain qualifications. Not only does one have to be a Christian, as is true with spiritual gifts, but a mature Christian (1 Tim. 3:2–13; Titus 1:5–9).

The differences between spiritual gifts and the offices of the church are evident. Every believer will have one or more spiritual gifts but may never occupy a church office. Believers do not need to seek spiritual gifts but do need to seek an office, at least the office of elder. And the only qualification for spiritual gifts is faith in Christ, whereas specific qualifications need to be met to hold an office.

Many confuse offices with gifts. For example, confusion exists between the gift of pastor and the office of pastor. The reason for this is the common practice in most churches of being led by an individual called a pastor. Actually this is a cultural phenomenon, not a biblical imperative. A thorough search of the Scriptures reveals that this practice is not biblical. That does not mean that it is wrong or should be abandoned, only that its practice cannot be defended from the Bible. This would be true of much of what takes place in the typical evangelical church on Sunday morning. Much of what churches do is dictated by the culture, not by Scripture.

Confusing gifts with offices affects your ministry vision. For example, many believe that the office of pastor in a church should be filled by a man and not a woman. From this they conclude that a woman could never be a pastor in a church. While it is true that a woman should not hold the office of pastor (or better, elder),[17] she may have the gift of pastor and exercise that gift in the local church, especially with the other women of the church. Most churches in North America desperately need women with pastoral gifts and a ministry vision to shepherd other women. A person with the gift of pastor, whether a man or woman, does not necessarily have to function as *the* pastor of a church but can shepherd people in a small group or any other context.

Whether the office of pastor must be filled by someone with the gift of pastor depends on the role the pastoral position plays in a particular church. In most small churches the pastor is expected to have shepherding skills because the people want to be nurtured. Small churches should seek someone with the gift of pastor and a pastoral ministry vision. In larger churches, however, the pastor is expected to be a leader, preacher, and teacher. He is not expected to literally shepherd all the people because the church is too large. Large churches should seek a man with the appropriate gifts and ministry vision.

Finally, a person's ministry design could include an office and spiritual gifts. This would be true of the office of elder. In Acts 20:28 and 1 Peter 5:1–2, the elders are told to pastor or shepherd God's people. While the gift of pastor is not necessarily a requirement, its presence in the individual enhances his performance dramatically.

Vocational Versus Nonvocational Ministry

In general, the terms *vocational* and *nonvocational* when used of ministry do not distinguish between those who have received a divine call and those who have not (according to the discussion above). Instead I use the terms in this book to distinguish between those who work regularly in that ministry and those who do not.

This involves several components. One is time. Often the terms *full-time* and *part-time* are used of a person's involvement in ministry. If the majority of your time is spent in the ministry rather than another vocation, then you are considered full-time. But if the majority of your time is not spent in that ministry, then it is part-time.

Another component is income. Those in vocational ministry derive their chief income from that ministry. Those in nonvocational ministry look to other sources for their primary income, such as the legal profession or the construction industry. Nevertheless, a lawyer or a carpenter should consider their professions as ministries for the Lord. Here the traditional line drawn between the sacred and the secular blurs. Certainly the construction skills of Bezalel and Oholiab were used for the Lord (Exod. 36:1–3). Consequently the distinction is not found necessarily in the Bible but in the attitudes and expectations of both Christians and non-Christians toward the ministry and their professions in general.

In terms of your ministry vision, you must make two decisions. First, do you desire to spend the majority of your time pursuing your ministry vision or only part of your time? Second, will you receive your income primarily from the pursuit of your ministry vision or some other source? For those who believe in a divine call to ministry, the answer depends on whether or not you have received that call. If you do not believe in a divine, inner call, the answer to both questions can be more difficult. For some ministry visions, few if any paid positions exist, and the answer is simple. An example would be a woman with the gift of pastor in a small church.

Answering these questions is more difficult when you consider positions involving remuneration. If every Christian left the work world to pursue a full-time ministry in the local church, the results would be disastrous. The same would hold true if the example is reversed. I suggest you determine the area in which you believe you can have the greatest impact for the Savior—your job or your ministry.

Worksheet

1. Would you categorize yourself as an active or nominal Christian? Why? Are you one of the "employed" who is involved in ministry, or among the "unemployed"? If you are among the "unemployed," what is the reason?

2. What does the Bible say about why you exist? Do you agree with that? Why or why not?

3. What is your church's philosophy of ministry (its core values)? What is your philosophy of ministry (your core values)? What effect can that have on your ministry? How does your philosophy of ministry relate to your ministry vision?

4. What is the biblical mission of the church? Is this your church's mission? What is your ministry mission? Have you begun the process of writing it down? How does it relate to your purpose? What is the difference between your ministry mission and your ministry vision?

5. Do you believe that God issues a distinct, inner call to those who are to go into vocational ministry? Why or why not? Have you received such a call? If so, describe it.

6. What is a paradigm? Is your church an old or new paradigm ministry according to this chapter? What is your paradigm preference? Why?

7. What is the difference between a church and a parachurch (or para-local church) ministry? Do you plan to minister in a church or parachurch ministry? Why? Name some of the advantages and disadvantages you will face in this ministry.

8. What is the difference between a vocational and a nonvocational ministry? Do you plan to pursue vocational or nonvocational ministry? Why?

The Discovery of 6
Your Personal Vision

What Is Your Ministry?

Although Tom did not realize it at the time, the discovery of his spiritual gifts was just the starting point. The purpose of the Bible study in the dorm was to uncover more than spiritual gifts; it was to help college students discover their divine design and then determine their personal ministry vision. The Christian organization that sponsored the campus Bible study highly valued this concept, and so it brought in a specialist who lived in the community to teach and work with the students in this area.

As a result Tom saw the rest of the pieces of his "puzzle" fall into place. Not only did he identify his spiritual gifts, he also discovered his passion, temperament, leadership abilities, and some natural gifts. The next step in the process, according to the specialist, was to determine his personal ministry vision—what he would do with his God-given design. There are two chronological steps to discovering your personal ministry vision: the vision identification step and the vision confirmation step.

The Identification of Your Personal Ministry Vision

The identification step helps you determine as precisely as possible your personal ministry vision. Most likely it will not pen down your exact vision, but it will provide you with a process for someday zeroing in on that vision. It consists of two phases that I will handle separately but that, in fact, work together. One focuses on ministry positions and the other on ministry people.

Ministry Positions

The focus on ministry positions involves two vital concepts: ministry matching and ministry projecting.

Ministry Matching

Ministry matching starts with the various positions in the ministry organization and matches them to the personal ministry design of the individual. For example, a local church may be adding a small-group program to its ministry menu and needs people to lead and shepherd those groups. First, it focuses on the ministry position of a small-group leader, drawing up a reasonably detailed ministry description (similar to a job description) that consists of the necessary spiritual gifts, passion, temperament, and so on needed for this ministry. Then it will seek someone with a design that most closely matches the small-group leader's ministry description.

Matching presumes that two important events have already taken place. First, the ministry organization needs to have identified its ministry positions and drawn up precise ministry descriptions for each position. The church will do much more than announce in the bulletin, "We have an immediate opening for a Sunday school teacher with the junior high girls." Willow Creek Community Church in northwest Chicago has developed a ministry description for each of the ministries in the church. This ministry description contains a concise statement of what the person is to do, the necessary spiritual gifts, the passion, the minimum spiritual maturity requirements, any needed talents and abilities, the preferred Myers-Briggs temperament (such as ENTP or ISTJ), the ministry target (adults, children), the necessary time commitment, and where the ministry will take place. To this could be added the score on the Biblical or Personal Profile.

This is a critical process that will make it more likely that Christ's people will be mobilized and have an effective ministry (Eph. 4:11–12). All too often the rule of thumb is to fill a slot with a warm body. For example, a church that has an opening on its leadership board will often fill that position with an individual who has been faithful in attending the church services and has shown an interest in the church's affairs. Instead the church should look for a Christian with the spiritual/natural gifts of leadership since the position calls for a leader. Those who are responsible for finding people for ministry must carefully and thoughtfully articulate the kind of design necessary to accomplish that ministry with maximum effectiveness and Christlikeness. If there is no one who comes close, then the organization is not ready for that particular ministry. When it is, Christ will raise up the right person with the right design.

Second, the ministry organization needs to have implemented an effective program for discovering the believer's divine design. It is the key to the mobilization and assimilation of its people. The program might consist of three stages.[1] The first is education that will provide believers in the ministry with instruction on the various divine design elements (as found in chapter 3) and then help them determine their personal ministry vision (as in this chapter). The second stage is consultation, in which people meet with a lay or professional person who provides personal ministry consultation one-on-one or in a small group. The third stage is mobilization, as the consultant helps believers determine where they can minister within the ministry organization.

Ministry Projecting

Ministry projecting also helps in determining your ministry vision. You should practice both ministry projecting and ministry matching because the two work together in determining your best ministry fit. Ministry projecting involves projecting from your divine design to your ministry position. Contrary to ministry matching, it begins with the person and then looks to the position. You examine each piece of your completed ministry puzzle (spiritual gifts, passion, and so on) and attempt to project or determine what God might do with it in a ministry context. In essence, you build the position around the person. Your design from God dictates your direction for God.

Your ministry design translates into your ministry style, and every style is unique. Adopting another's exact ministry model is a grave mistake. For example, to mimic Billy Graham's evangelistic ministry would most likely result in failure even if you have practically the same design. Because of your uniqueness, you must allow your ministry model to take shape based on your design. Pastors who are planting or revitalizing churches in one part of the country often attempt to replicate a popular, successful church in another, hoping for the same success. There are numerous problems with that. One is that it is not authentic and does not flow from the leader's own style but from that of another. While we can learn certain principles from others' ministries, we face dire consequences if we copy them.

When projecting your personal ministry vision, you may discover a single, precise vision such as leading and preaching in an evangelistic organization. However, you might also discover your vision includes several related ministry positions. The concept of ministry range can be helpful in this process (see figure 5). A ministry range consists of the various ministries (represented by the crosses) in a particular ministry organization on a continuum with the ministries that make up your best fit on the extreme left, a questionable fit in the center, and no fit on the extreme right.

Ministry Range

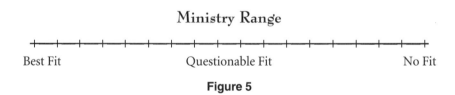

Best Fit   Questionable Fit   No Fit

Figure 5

It is possible, as the best-fit area shows in figure 5, that several related ministry positions fall within your ministry vision. One lay person might discover that she could best serve the Savior in a church as a greeter on Sunday mornings and as a volunteer counselor two evenings each month. Another might discover he could serve Christ full-time by functioning as the senior pastor in a church or by teaching homiletics (preaching), church leadership, and other ministry topics in a seminary setting. He would need to decide which he prefers to pursue.

After projecting your preferred ministry position, you may discover your church or ministry organization does not have a position that accommodates your specific design but would benefit greatly from it. Pray about asking the ministry's leaders to create a new ministry position.

Ministry People

The concept of ministry people moves from the ministry position to the ministry person. It focuses not on the various ministry positions but on the person who is ministering well in a particular ministry position. It is person-centered, not ministry-centered. Employing the ministry people concept in addition to or along with the ministry positions concept aids you even further in detecting your personal ministry vision.

The Concept

The ministry people concept looks to particular individuals whom God has chosen to bless in a particular ministry over the years. It is obvious by what God is accomplishing through them that they have found their ministry visions.

On the one hand, they may be as well-known as Billy Graham, Chuck Swindoll, Mother Teresa, Charles Colson, E. V. Hill, Elisabeth Elliot, Bill Bright, James Dobson, Anthony Evans, or Joni Eareckson Tada. On the other hand, they may be known only in a particular area, or they may not be well-known at all. Most likely, a ministry person is someone in a church: the pastor, a godly lay leader, or the church custodian. It would be a mistake to assume that those who are well-known are more spiritual or faithful than those who are not. God has seen fit in his sovereignty to allow the public spotlight to shine on some and not on others. We must take care when considering well-known ministry figures. Be aware of your motives. Does your design and vision truly come close to that person's, or are you trying to be someone you are not? Many seminarians would love to have a ministry like that of Chuck Swindoll for a variety of reasons—some good and some not so good. But there is only one Chuck Swindoll.

The ministry people concept looks at the designs of the person in focus, in particular the ones that are most like yours. Based on the similarity of designs, it considers whether the ministry visions are similar as well. You might have the gifts of evangelism, leadership, and preaching. Sound familiar? That is the point! Since you and Billy Graham have the same gifts, the possibility exists that you might have similar ministry visions. Or you might discover that you have the same gifts as your pastor, the director of the church's drama team, or the lady who serves as the part-time counselor.

Consequently you could carefully probe their ministries to discover if your ministry vision is the same or similar to theirs.

Another example is a dynamic, church planting pastor. You are aware of his ministry because of the impact it is having on the unchurched, lost people in your community. Many have come to Christ and been discipled, including the mayor. As you investigate this pastor's divine design, you discover you have much in common—the same approximate gifts, passion, temperament, and so on. The concept of ministry people teaches that in light of this affinity you should prayerfully consider leading a church planting team in a ministry similar to the one just described. It is also quite possible that God may use you similarly—but differently—because of some divine design differences. Regardless, you have benefitted in the personal vision process and saved time.

Where the ministry people concept is most effective and beneficial for determining your ministry vision is in the ministries that do a good job overall in helping all their people to discover their designs and ministry visions. Most likely these will be organizations that employ a program such as the instruction, consultation, and implementation stages mentioned above, requiring it of all their people or at least making it available to them. The advantage is those responsible for this ministry will have an awareness of or information on all the people with the same or similar designs and will use them as potential indicators of personal ministry vision.

The Research

Recently those thinking and working in the field of assessment have made some significant contributions to the concept of ministry people. Most research has focused on those in two full-time, vocational ministries: church revitalization and church planting. Much of the church ministry that will take place in the late 1990s and the twenty-first century will be in these two areas.

Church revitalization. Robert Thomas has written a doctoral dissertation attempting to answer the question "What types of personality traits are characteristic of an effective revitalization pastor?"[2] Among other things, the study sought to develop a working profile for use in identifying and placing pastors designed for the ministry of revitalizing churches.[3]

In his survey of twenty Baptist General Conference pastors (ministry people) who had a proven record of renewing churches, Thomas used the Biblical Personal Profile to isolate their specific personality or temperament characteristics. He discovered that of fifteen possible patterns, all the effective revitalization pastors he studied fell within one: the persuader pattern.[4] The profile supplies the following temperament description:

> Persuaders work with and through people. That is, they strive to do business in a friendly way while pushing forward to win their own objectives. Possessing an outgoing interest in people, Persuaders have the ability to gain the respect and confidence of various types of individuals. This ability is particularly helpful to Persuaders in winning positions of authority. In addition, they seek work assignments which provide opportunities to make them look good. Work with people, challenging assignments, variety of work and activities which require mobility provide the most favorable environment for Persuaders. However, they may be too optimistic about the results of projects and the potential of people. Persuaders also tend to overestimate their ability to change the behavior of others. While Persuaders seek freedom from routine and regimentation, they do need to be supplied with analytical data on a systematic basis. When they are alerted to the importance of "little things," adequate information helps them to control impulsiveness.[5]

The value of Thomas's work is that the Biblical Personal Profile or the Personal Profile can be used to help pastors determine if their ministry designs are conducive to a ministry vision of renewing established churches.[6] Voges writes, "The Biblical Personal Profile (BPP) measures behavioral tendencies. It is not meant to be a prescriptive tool. You and others do not 'have to behave' like your profile. *However, it is a fairly accurate predictive tool. You will 'tend' to behave as described.*"[7]

Church planting. In *Planting Growing Churches for the 21st Century*, one chapter asks, "Are You a Church Planter?"[8] While a number of designs are suitable for those who would be part of a church planting team, there is a unique design for those who would plant solo or serve as the point person on a team. This design includes such spiritual gifts as leadership, faith, evangelism, and preaching.[9] Their passion is often for lost people in general and unchurched, lost people in particular. On the Biblical or Personal Profile and Indicator 1 in appendix B, they tend to be high "I"s or Ds or a combination of the two.

The Christian Churches/Disciples of Christ performed a survey using the Personal Profile to correlate the personality types of sixty-six church planters (ministry people) with the growth of their churches. The survey revealed that the high D planters had an average attendance of seventy-two after the first year and 181 after an average of 5.2 years. The high "I"s had an average of ninety-eight after the first year and an average of 174 after 3.6 years. The high Ss had an average of thirty-eight after the first year and seventy-seven after 6.3 years, while the high Cs had an average of thirty-nine after one year and seventy-one after 4.3 years.[10] This reveals that if church planting success is to be measured in terms of reaching and ministering to people, then the "I"s and Ds have the edge when planting either by themselves or leading a team of church planters.

There are some additional design elements. In terms of leadership, solo church planters are leader-managers in their roles and either autocratic, democratic, or a combination of the two in their styles.[11]

Robert Thomas makes the following insightful comment on the use of the Biblical Personal Profile for those anticipating full-time ministry:

> This profile has been said to meet a major need for many denominational executives. The development of other operational profiles could further assist them in the difficult task of screening candidates for ministry. Suggested areas for further study are a church planter profile, an interim pastor profile, a small, medium, and large church pastor's profile, and an associate minister's profile. It is interesting that the few large church pastor profiles this writer observed were all "task oriented," "High 'D'" profiles. It is quite likely there are different personalities for each of the suggested areas of need.[12]

The need, however, is for similar work to be done in the areas of ministry vision inhabited largely by lay people. The limited amount of research thus far has focused on professional ministry. Research in lay ministry areas as well will prove vital to mobilizing the full body of Christ for powerful, significant ministry in the twenty-first century.

The Confirmation of Your Personal Ministry Vision

While the identification step serves to help you discover your ministry vision, the confirmation step seeks to validate the accuracy of your discovery.

It consists of three phases that are distinct but work together to confirm your ministry vision.

The Observation Phase

The observation phase involves self-observation based on the knowledge of your past consistent behavior. You carefully examine the results of the identification process and ask yourself, Is this true of me? Is this what I think I can do? The reason why this phase is so important is we are the ones who ultimately determine the accuracy of any phase of any assessment program. We can use highly sophisticated tools, such as the Biblical Personal Profile or Myers-Briggs Type Indicator, to determine our design, but they only reflect the information we give. If the information for our vision is based on what we want to do or what someone else thinks we should do, then at best it tells us nothing and at worst it leads us astray. Next to our omniscient God, we are the ones who know ourselves best. As we weigh the results of all assessment, it is our responsibility to determine its accuracy based on our self-observation.

However, there exists the ever present problem of subjectivity. We are working on the basis of how we feel or what we think. For various reasons we have the potential to distort the information. Two other phases help us detect this: the consultation and experimentation phases.

The Consultation Phase

The consultation phase involves intentionally seeking and accepting wise counsel and advice regarding the accuracy of your ministry vision. Its purpose is to confirm or correct your ministry vision through the help and input of other significant people. This phase is not temporary but will last a lifetime because of the constant need to evaluate and refine the direction of our ministries in light of additional personal insight and ministry experience. It should consume much time and energy initially and then gradually decrease in intensity over the years.

The Importance of Consultation

Scripture advises us to seek the counsel and advice of wise people. Proverbs 15:22 says, "Plans fail for lack of counsel, but with many advisers they succeed." The counsel of others most often brings wisdom. Proverbs 19:20 advises, "Listen to advice and accept instruction, and in the end you will be wise." Other passages encourage the same (Prov. 12:15; 13:14, 20; 20:18; 24:5–6; 27:9).

Getting counsel adds an objective element to what otherwise can be a subjective experience. We may carry a hidden agenda and not be aware of it. We may rationalize and distort the feedback we receive from the various indicators and tools because we want to be or do something other than what we have been designed to be and do. Wise counsel serves to offset and correct this problem.

A third reason for consultation is some people are confused as to who they really are. They may have grown up in a situation where they were pressured to be who they were not. Paul and Barbara Tieger explain, "Children are particularly vulnerable to others' expectations and often suppress their own natural preferences in order to fit in and be accepted."[13] Again they write, "Children who are discouraged from using their innate strengths can grow up to be confused and ambivalent about their perceptions and inclinations—and this confusion can affect every aspect of adult life, including career issues."[14] Other people can see through all this and help them discover their true identity.

The Sources for Consultation

We must seek advice from the right people, however. Good counselors display several characteristics. First, they are people who know you reasonably well. High on the list is your spouse. Your husband or wife may know you better than any other person in your life, and so I suggest you have your spouse also take the indicators (located in the appendixes) on you. If the results are similar to or the same as yours, then you probably have an accurate feel for who you are. If they differ, then you would be wise to discuss these differences and possibly repeat the process. The same holds true for the confirmation of your ministry vision. Other people who could prove helpful as advisors are your parents, close friends, children, and pastor.

A second source of good counsel is those involved in a ministry similar to that for which you have a vision. Since these people are serving in the ministry firsthand, they can give you an idea of all that is involved. Often we only see the surface of a work, or what we want to see. We have no idea what goes on behind the scenes. Thus our picture of a ministry may be distorted or entirely inaccurate. Spending some time interacting with those in the ministry should help us catch reality and gives them an opportunity to get to know us and determine if we are a good fit for that ministry.

A third source is Christians who have demonstrated unusual wisdom into life and who display keen insight into people. They have the unusual ability to see things in you that others, including you, may not see. They can not only confirm obvious gifts and talents but spot dormant abilities and bring them to our attention so we can cultivate them in ministry for Christ.

A fourth source for confirming your ministry vision is people who are truth-tellers. Truth-tellers don't tell you what they think you want to hear or what you actually do want to hear. They tell you the truth. Some will speak the truth with love; others will tell you the truth with little regard for your feelings. While they come across as harsh, they are doing you a favor. Do not make the mistake of rejecting their counsel because of how they communicate their thoughts.

A fifth source is people who are on your side. In general, you want to pursue those who have your best interests at heart, who are "on your team." They desire God's very best for you not only in life in general but your ministry in particular.

A sixth source of confirmation is the consultant. Some churches have begun to use consultants—either from within or outside the congregation—in mobilizing their people for ministry. If this is your situation, consider yourself blessed and use their services. If this is not your situation, look for a church in your community or nearby that does use a lay or professional consultant.

The Questions for Consultants

When you seek the counsel and advice of another person, you should ask certain specific questions. One is, What do you see me doing or not doing with my life? The words *doing* and *not doing* will help them approach the issue from two sides. The same question asked differently is, If you were in my shoes with my design, how would you serve Christ? Once you have asked a question, sit back and let them talk. Resist interrupting them except to clarify any points you do not understand. You may have to prod them at first. Let them know you want to hear the truth whatever that may be. By doing this you give them permission to relax and be truth-tellers.

After they're finished, say something like "I'm thinking about pursuing a certain ministry. I value your opinion and want to know what you think. In your opinion, would I make a good Sunday school teacher of adults (leader for a small group, campus evangelist, a pastor of a church)?" Watch for visual cues while listening to their words. They may say one thing and signal another. When this is the case, seek further counsel from others.

A third question is, Why do you feel the way you do about my ministry vision? The reason behind their positive or negative response may be as important as the response itself. For example, a trusted friend may counsel you not to pursue vocational ministry as a campus evangelist at the present. The reason: "You are task-oriented, and evangelism requires someone with developed people skills. Wait a year or two until you have had more time to further develop your people skills."

The Experimentation Phase

Pursuing the counsel and wisdom of others to confirm your ministry vision should prove most valuable. A third complementary phase involves experimenting with your vision by getting ministry experience.

The Value of Experimentation

Ministry experience supplies "seasoning." It is one thing to think and talk with others about your direction; it is another to experience it. You need to spend some time experiencing your ministry niche before claiming ownership. You don't know for sure if you can drive a car just by listening to a lecture in a driver's education class. The true test comes when you slip behind the wheel and get out on the road.

As you involve yourself in a ministry, you should feel a sense of significance and fulfillment in at least 60 percent of what you do. If you drop below 50 percent, chances are good you will experience burnout and will eventually drop out. This does not mean your ministry vision will be problem-free. Every ministry has its "bedpans." However, when you are in the right ministry, even the bedpans seem easier to clean, and the problems are less threatening.

Options

Those considering professional ministries in a church or parachurch should pursue an internship. The general rule is the longer the internship the higher the learning curve. The shortest internship should be equivalent to a semester of school—about four to six months or a summer. However, this is minimal and works best in quality organizations that place a premium on training men and women for ministry. The best internships last from one to two years because this period of time allows the ministry seasoning process to take place.

Lay people need experience as well. Bruce Bugbee suggests giving people three opportunities. If the first is not the right ministry fit, then the person can try the second, and third. Each ministry is responsible to train a new person "on the job." If no position is suitable to someone's design, then a new ministry could be designed around that person.

Suggestions

For ministry experience to prove valuable in confirming your vision, it must take place with the right people in the right context. As with seeking wise counsel and advice, not just any ministry will do. I will briefly mention several factors that are further developed in the next chapter (under Practical Suggestions for Ministry-Based Training). First, seek a quality ministry organization. You want to be trained in the best situation possible. Second, seek a ministry that fits your ministry vision. If you plan to minister in a new paradigm church, then do your training in a similar situation. Third, look for a ministry staff that is committed to training its people. Fourth, agree on the expectations of the trainer and trainee in advance. This will prevent major problems later on. Fifth, develop a ministry training plan. Without a clear, personalized plan you will waste your time and others'.

Worksheet

1. Does the ministry you are a part of have a detailed ministry description for its key ministry positions? If not, why not?

2. Does your ministry have a program for helping people discover their divine designs? If yes, how effective is it? If not, why not?

3. Are you aware of most of the ministry positions in your church or parachurch? As you practice ministry matching, what ministry position(s) best matches your ministry design?

4. Based on your divine design, project the kind of ministry you should pursue. Does your ministry organization have such a position? If not, is it willing to start one?

5. Do you know of a person or persons whom God is blessing in ministry who has a divine design similar to yours? What is his or her ministry? Do you feel an affinity for that kind of ministry?

6. If you are considering vocational pastoral ministry, is your design similar to that of a pastor involved in church renewal or church planting? Is your ministry vision church renewal or church planting?

7. At this point in your discovery process, what is your ministry vision? Have you written it down on paper? No matter how accurate your statement, it is most important that you begin the process of writing it out as soon as you finish this chapter. It may go through a number of revisions, but that is part of the process of articulating a significant personal ministry vision. Use the format provided by the examples in chapter 5 as your initial guide.

8. Have you consulted with anyone regarding the confirmation of your ministry vision? If not, why not? If yes, who? Do they meet the qualifications for a good source of counsel? What was their response?

9. What ministry experiences are available to help you confirm your ministry vision? What is the attitude of those in these ministries toward working with you? In light of your design, which is the best possible ministry environment to test your vision? Has any experience thus far either confirmed or contradicted your vision?

$Part$ 3

Directing Your
Personal Development
for Ministry

The last part of this book will help you accomplish or realize your personal ministry vision. Now that you know who you are (your ministry identity) and what God wants you to do (your ministry vision), the third and final step in the process focuses on your ministry development. It answers the question, How do I best prepare for my ministry or range of ministries? The answer is to design a unique ministry training plan.

The Concept and Contents of a Training Plan

What Can You Learn from a Professor or a Pastor?

David is now back at the seminary. He spends much of his time in the library quietly doing research in preparation for his doctoral courses. Sometimes he thinks he has died and gone to heaven. He loves what he is doing, and God is providing for his family's material needs. The company where his wife worked during his prior studies rehired her and increased her salary substantially. Since they have no children, they should be able to get by financially until he completes his program.

The last two years in the pastorate have proved profitable. Not only has God used this time to direct him to the teaching ministry, but David has gained practical ministry knowledge, experience, and some ministry skills. Enough that he has been invited to preach regularly at a small church located thirty miles from downtown.

Through the knowledge of his ministry design and the discovery of his ministry vision, David knows that much of his ministry preparation will involve classroom-based education. He is preparing for a professional ministry that requires a graduate degree from an accredited theological institution.

But what ministry preparation is necessary for Tom and lay people like Carol to realize their personal ministry dreams? Actually David, Tom, and Carol are far ahead of many in the process. Most Christians work through the process in reverse order. They know they want to serve the Lord but are not sure how. So they begin the process with the preparation stage hoping that somewhere along the way they will find their personal ministry visions. They may enroll in a Christian college or seminary even though they have no future ministry vision or an ill-defined, inaccurate one. Because so little information is available on the divine design concept, they may never have considered the design stage and have not discovered their gifts, temperaments, and natural abilities.

David, Tom, and Carol are ahead in the process because they have taken each step in the proper order. First, they discovered their divine designs for ministry (chapters 1–4). Next, based on those designs, they determined their personal ministry visions (chapters 5–6). Now it is time for them to take the third step—ministry development (chapters 7–8)—which involves preparing a ministry plan.

But what is the concept behind this plan? And what are its contents?

The Concept of the Plan

In light of who you are (your design), how can you best prepare to accomplish your personal ministry vision (your direction)? You can answer that question by designing a lifetime personal training plan tailor-made for your individual ministry situation. That is the concept behind the development stage. This plan is designed to take you from wherever you are and move you to where you want to be in ministry.

Your Plan Assumes Your Divine Design

First, a personal training plan assumes you have a reasonable knowledge of your ministry design. This depends on where you are in the design discovery process. Some people know themselves well. They have always been sensitive and alert to who they are. Thus they are ahead in the process. Others, however, do not know themselves as well. For a number of reasons they may not have been as observant, so they are behind in the process. These people are often late bloomers. They discover their design and become productive in ministry later in life. Others look at them and are amazed at the change. This often contributes to the mistaken view that people can change their temperaments, when, in reality, they are just discovering and realizing their true identity. Regardless of whether you are advanced in the divine design process or a little behind, you are so unique and wonderfully made that you will continue to discover and refine your design for the rest of your life.

Your Plan Assumes Your Ministry Vision

Second, the development of your ministry plan assumes a reasonable knowledge of your ministry direction (your personal vision). Since the discovery and development of your design is an ongoing process, you will need to regularly refine and adjust your vision. It is like focusing a movie projector on a screen. Time is on your side. The longer you think about and work with the concepts in this book, the clearer they become. Keep in mind that this is a process that does not take place overnight.

Your Plan Prepares You for Your Ministry

With a reasonable knowledge of your ministry design and direction, you are ready to pursue your ministry development. Everyone needs preparation. Even if you are an unusually gifted person, you are aware of your present need for ministry development. And this, too, does not take place overnight. Like the discovery of your design and vision, it takes time and hard work. A man with the natural talent to play the piano needs to take lessons and practice regularly. A woman with the gift of evangelism will need some instruction and experience in sharing her faith.

Most likely you have already given your ministry development some thought. In fact you may have unknowingly begun the process at this point rather than with the design and direction phases. For example, you may be in school with little idea of your design or direction. If this is the case, you may need to make some minor adjustments or major changes. You may have thought that God wanted you to be an accountant, but now realize he has designed you to pastor a church. You are enrolled in business school, preparing to be a CPA. You may need to leave school and pursue seminary training. Others may need to leave seminary and begin training to become a CPA, farmer, or plumber.

Not only does everyone need preparation, they need to think in terms of a lifetime of preparation. Those who are serious about serving the Savior, whether lay or professional, need to tailor a lifetime training program. All too often churches and schools look at training as "front end" preparation, as introductory, as if those in ministry had somehow arrived and have no further need for development.

Church and parachurch ministries may take pride in the fact that they provide training for their people—although many in their ranks have not even progressed this far. How often is a recently recruited third grade Sunday school teacher still simply handed a lesson book and pointed in the direction of the class? Still, many who have progressed beyond this point fail to see the need for lifetime continuing education. David Ludeker writes of the professional minister: "The passivity of clergy in planning learning goals is widely known. There is a heresy in the American culture which has permeated the Church: 'that professional training ends with entry training.' The result is that many clergy fail to see the need of planning a life-time program of learning."[1]

Lay and professional people who are serious about ministry must take charge of the process of tailoring a lifelong training program that will equip them for their various ministry positions. In light of the speed of change at the end of the twentieth century, this planning is more short- than long-range. This calls for periodic planning and replanning throughout our lifetime as circumstances change. Life is too short to wait on churches or schools to offer the necessary programs; instead we must proactively plan and seek the necessary training.

The Contents of the Plan

What are the contents of a good, tailor-made plan for ministry that will serve you for a lifetime? The primary or essential contents of your plan are the three Cs: your life circumstances, ministry competencies, and training contexts. The first two answer the question *what* and the last answers the question *where*. (Other contents of the plan that answer the questions *who*, *when*, and *how* will be discussed in chapter 8.)

Your Life Circumstances

No one lives in a vacuum. Everyone exists in a particular situation that affects to a great degree who they are and what they do in life. The effect these circumstances have on our ministries cannot be overstated. In your ministry plan, the primary emphasis falls on your ministry competencies and training contexts. However, both are poured through and influenced by the grid of your life circumstances. Chapter 2 listed some circumstances, but there are others, and all are important to the planning process. The following circumstances are explored in more detail in chapter 8.

Your Age

While you are never too young or too old to serve Christ, your age will affect your ministry plan, especially as you decide between lay or professional ministry. Most ministries have room for lay workers regardless of their age. However, many prefer someone between their thirties and fifties for professional service.

Your Marital and Family Status

Three family factors play an important role in planning for a lifetime of ministry. First, if you are single, you have much freedom in your ministry pursuits, but most ministries prefer married people over singles. Second, if you are married, spousal cooperation and the age of your children play an important part. Finally, if you have been divorced, you may face some obstacles in ministry, especially as a professional.

Your Prior Education

Everyone must have a basic education upon which to build their ministry. It affects their ministry ability and credibility. Again a person in lay ministry is granted more lenience than a professional. Regardless, the higher your education, the greater the opportunities you will have for ministry at all levels.

Your Gender

Most women serve on a lay level. Also the majority of women minister in the area of Christian education with children from birth to adolescence. However, with new ministry paradigms springing up, women are ministering in other areas. For example, women with the gift of pastor are leading and ministering in small groups for women.

Your Health and Any Disabilities

The health of your family is a factor, including both your immediate family (especially your spouse and children) and your extended family. A problem in any of these areas, whether physical or emotional, can have serious impact on your ministry because of your time and availability. Another factor is a disability. A physical disability does not have to curtail the exercise of your giftedness, depending on the ministry organization with which you serve. Some have found their greatest ministry opportunities are with others who have a similar disability.

Your Finances

Training for professional ministry can be expensive, while training for lay ministries is usually inexpensive. The former has resulted in fewer men and women pursuing professional ministry positions. The latter has resulted in some people not valuing their ministry preparation.

All of the above life circumstances will affect your ministry plan to some degree. As you examine your ministry competencies and training contexts, you must weigh their influence in any developmental plan.

Your Ministry Competencies

Competency and authenticity in ministry walk hand in hand. Christians who are incompetent at what they do are inauthentic, and as a result people will not trust them. You would not trust an incompetent heart surgeon with your life, no matter how good his or her character. Therefore all who serve Christ must strive for competency in that sphere of service. I see a need for competence in three critical areas. One is your personal character, which is the foundation of your ministry. The second is the knowledge base necessary for understanding your ministry. And the third is the appropriate skills to accomplish your ministry.

The Development of Your Character

An authentic ministry development plan starts with the ongoing development of your character. You must begin with the character question: Who do I need to be? As briefly stated in chapter 2, for you to be effective in any ministry, *being* (character) precedes *doing* (ministry). We cannot drive far on an empty tank. God accomplishes through us what he has accomplished in us. To do otherwise is to be guilty of what Howard Hendricks describes as "trafficking in unlived truth." While it is not necessary that you have personally experienced everything you address in ministry, it is crucial that you have experienced an authentic walk with God.

It is possible to discover your divine design and direction for ministry and fail to cultivate your heart and soul for the same. It is exciting to discover your God-given spiritual gifts and talents, begin to minister with them, and have a significant impact in people's lives. However, it is easy to be distracted by all this and allow your soul to shrivel in the process. Initially the result of such a ministry approach is ministry burnout, which is God's early warning system. Failure to take note and respond appropriately will in time result in ministry dropout.

God does not use and abuse his people. He desires to accomplish a work in your life that will supply all you need to minister in the lives of others. As you have an enduring impact on others, he desires to have an enduring impact on you. Therefore time must be set aside in your life to develop your character as well as employ your gifts, talents, and abilities.

This can take place in two contexts. The first is private and individual. It involves a hearty, robust quiet time alone with God. The Savior has set the example (see Mark 1:35; Luke 6:12; and 9:18). This time usually includes prayer, worship, and Bible study.

The second is public and corporate. It is a mistake to emphasize the devotional approach to the exclusion of the community approach. By itself the devotional, private approach can feed the independent and competitive appetite that already predominates ministry preparation and practice. But Christ accomplishes far more in community than in private. This includes spiritual formation in such contexts as mentoring, small groups, and public worship that incorporates the proclamation of Scripture.

The Development of Your Knowledge Base

A realistic ministry development plan also includes the expansion of your knowledge base for ministry. What do you need to know? While *being* (character) must precede *doing* (ministry), *knowing* (content) must walk hand in hand with *doing*. On the one hand, there is the problem of training people in the classroom for ministry (classroom-based learning) without the balance of experience in the field (ministry-based training). This circumstance plagues those preparing for professional ministry exclusively in Christian colleges and seminaries. On the other hand, there exists the problem of involving people in ministry without an adequate knowledge base. This problem affects both the lay and professional person who pursues ministry without sufficient knowledge to be competent at what they do. These people learn how to minister by trial and error, which is roughly analogous to learning how to drive by having a series of accidents. Neither is satisfactory and both can prove painful.

What kind of knowledge complements experience? Christ's servants must have a working knowledge in a variety of areas. One is a knowledge of the Scriptures. The Bible is the source of divine truth that speaks authoritatively to the believer's faith and practice. All believers need to know the content and message of the Bible as well as to master basic Bible study skills. A second area is a basic knowledge of theology.

Along with a knowledge of the Bible and theology you need a knowledge of people for competent ministry to take place. You can accomplish this by becoming a student of people and pursuing studies on temperament. I suggest you begin by reading some of the books on temperament listed in chapter 4.

Finally, you will need a knowledge of the ministry essentials for your specific ministry direction. First, you will need to become aware of what the ministry essentials are in general (several are listed in chapter 8), and then you will need to refine those that are essential and unique to your ministry vision. For example, a second grade Sunday school teacher will profit by having a knowledge of Christian education in general, but even more from a knowledge of how to disciple second graders in particular. A leader of a small group should know something about the small-group process. A church planter should know something about the principles and process of church planting.

The Development of Your Skills

Finally, the ministry plan includes the acquisition and development of the skills necessary to accomplish ministry. The skills question is, What do I need to do? Many fail to realize that the inability to exercise certain skills has as great a potential to knock us out of ministry as a lack of character or insufficient knowledge of the Bible. A pastor or lay leader in the church who lacks interpersonal skills may fail at ministry because so much of it is people-related.

A variety of skills will need the constant attention and development of Christ's servants: Bible study, communication (reading, writing, speaking, and listening), conflict resolution, problem solving, consensus building, planning and goal setting, meetings management, risk taking, role clarification, rewards and recognition, vision casting, networking, team building, group process, evaluation, time management, values clarification. These will be examined in greater detail in chapter 8.

Your Training Contexts

Where will you get the necessary training for competence in each of these areas? There are three primary sources for training in your personal ministry development plan. Two sources are classroom-based and ministry-based training. A third is supplementary training that complements the other two. In light of our present education-minded society, I have set aside the rest of this chapter to explore these three contexts in depth.

Classroom-Based Training

Tom, David, and lay people like Carol who are serious about ministry preparation benefit from classroom-based education. Normally this takes place in a Christian college or seminary setting. These schools primarily offer programs and training for those in pursuit of vocational ministry such as the pastorate, missions, teaching, and counseling. However, most Christian colleges and a growing number of seminaries have begun to offer special programs and advanced studies for those who are not pursuing a vocational Christian ministry but want further preparation for their ministries.

Those who are considering classroom-based education in their ministry training plans need to think through the advantages and disadvantages of going to school.

The advantages of classroom-based education. Classroom-based education has a number of decided advantages over other approaches to ministry training. Some of the more important advantages are training time, learning resources, biblical and theological studies, and ministry credentials.

1. *Training time.* One advantage of classroom-based preparation is the economy of your time—it condenses what could be many years of study into a shorter period of time. Thus it is more focused and intense. If you were to privately pursue studies in the areas that most college or seminary curriculums cover, it would take you two or three times as long to gain the same knowledge base. In addition, you would not have the same guidance in your studies that is provided by a competent faculty who in most institutions exert a major influence over the programs and curriculums.

Bible colleges and Christian liberal arts colleges provide various programs ranging from a one-year certificate to a four-year bachelor of arts or bachelor of science degree. Building on your degree from a secular institution, seminaries provide programs on the masters level from one to three years. They also offer doctoral programs that require three to four years for completion.

2. *Learning resources.* A second advantage of the classroom-based approach is the learning resources provided by the schools. One resource is the faculty members, who have been through extensive training in their fields of expertise. Since more teachers are available than teaching positions, the field has become very competitive. Colleges and seminaries make high requirements of their instructors: a doctoral degree, prior teaching experience, expertise in their field, and impeccable Christian character. This certainly works to the advantage of the student who needs and wants the best faculty person available for their training.

Another resource is the library. Accrediting institutions require that schools have libraries that meet high academic standards. A tremendous wealth of knowledge is available in one central location in the form of books, periodicals, abstracts, theses, journals, and tapes. The student can use the library to do extensive research into any biblical or theological topic, and the holdings of other libraries can be easily accessed by computer.

3. *Biblical and theological studies.* A third advantage is the pursuit of studies in biblical and theological areas. Evangelical colleges and seminaries focus on learning the Bible and its theology. The Christian liberal arts school seeks to provide its students with training in many of the same areas as a secular school, areas such as English, history, mathematics, physics, business, music. However, they accomplish this training within the context of an integrated Christian worldview. In addition, they usually offer some introductory courses and electives in Bible and theology. Those who finish their studies receive a bachelor's degree.

The Bible college seeks to provide its students with sound teaching in the Bible and theology on an undergraduate level. Though it may provide some introductory, foundational courses in areas such as English and history, its curriculum consists primarily of courses covering the books of the Bible, basic areas of theology, preaching, practical ministries, biblical languages, music, and counseling. Students who attend Bible colleges for four years generally use their studies as preparation for ministry or further studies in another academic environment such as the seminary. Those who complete their studies are awarded a bachelor's degree.

The theological seminary, like the Bible college, provides students with a sound knowledge of the Bible and theology but on a graduate level. Its curriculum is built on the foundation of an undergraduate degree. Therefore it assumes students have a satisfactory liberal arts education that has provided them with the basic skills to pursue graduate studies. The seminary curriculum is more advanced and provides classes that go farther and deeper than a Bible college. Those who complete seminary are awarded a master's or a doctoral degree.

4. *Ministry credentials.* A fourth advantage of classroom-based ministry preparation is it supplies you with the academic credentials necessary to pursue ministry credentials.

Christian organizations vary widely in their academic requirements for those who desire to be a part of their ministries. Many organizations do not require any college or seminary degree as a credential for ministry. The people who are responsible for these church or para-local church ministries like to have college-trained people, but it is not a necessary requirement to be involved in the work. You do not need a college degree to serve in a church on Sunday morning as a greeter, usher, bus driver, singer, or Sunday school teacher. While a seminary degree could enhance your ministry, you may not need one to function as a pastor whether the church is big or small. In his doctoral studies, Richard Olson discovered that "more than one-third of the senior ministers of megachurches did not hold a seminary degree."[2] Nor do you need one to serve in a parachurch organization, ministering to the poor, witnessing to ethnic groups, or counseling those in the military. However, most in these positions acknowledge that a good education does make a difference in the quality and depth of one's ministry.

Finally, a few ministry organizations exist that require some kind of degree to be involved in service. Some local churches, due to their size or denominational affiliation, also require a degree, and in some cases they want not only an undergraduate degree but a seminary degree. The faculties of most if not all schools need advanced degrees to qualify for their teaching positions. Though some nondegreed people may be just as highly qualified, accrediting organizations insist that most people who teach in an institution that grants an academic degree have an academic degree.

The disadvantages of classroom-based education. We live in a culture that values and emphasizes classroom-based education, as evidenced by the number of Christian and non-Christian educational institutions that exist in North America. However, this approach to preparation has several disadvantages. Those that are most evident are high costs, personal sacrifices, an academic emphasis, poor ministry exposure, and passive involvement.

1. *High costs.* Inflation and the rising deficit have deeply affected most colleges and universities across North America, as well as Christian colleges and seminaries. Due to fewer students and rising costs, a number of Christian liberal arts and Bible colleges have closed their doors. Others survive on a day-to-day basis. Those with substantial endowments or capable leaders have been able to keep pace with inflation and hold tuition costs down.

The extent to which seminaries can survive the economic climate is questionable. Tuition has risen at a remarkable rate in the last decade, reaching a point where students find it difficult to earn enough money to cover their educational expenses. Unfortunately many who would be students simply cannot afford what some feel is now a luxury. Those pursuing seminary studies often come with families that require additional income to cover all expenses, and most seminarians work in addition to going to school.

Most students are willing to bear their fair share of the costs of getting an education, and many will have to incur some debt to accomplish this. The problem is that the income you can expect from some ministries is low, and as a result it will take longer to repay debt. Hopefully, more churches will rise to the occasion and help those from their congregations who pursue advanced studies. Presently, not many churches have this kind of vision.

Thus students should carefully think through how they will fund their college or seminary studies. They should confer with the admission officers and counselors at their prospective schools and inquire about grants and loans. Often agencies and organizations exist in their hometowns that offer scholarships to students. Some states do the same. In certain situations a spouse can work without detriment to the family. The reality is that many students will have to work their way through school. What all students have going for them, however, is the truth that God provides (Prov. 3:5–6).

2. *Personal sacrifices.* The majority of students who want a college or seminary education have to pursue them at some personal sacrifice. It can take several different forms. One is a major move from a particular part of the country to another. While an increasing number of Christian colleges and seminaries have begun to establish extension centers in various cities across North America, not all have moved in this new direction, and so some students will have to leave family and friends as well as ministries to get an education. Not only is this expensive, new jobs in the location of the school usually come at a lower salary.

However, this situation exists only for a limited period of time. Students eventually will reach the end of their educational program and graduate. Just as students who pursue the fields of medicine and law have to make personal sacrifices, so do those in ministry for Christ. You have to pay a price for anything of value, like education. The question is, Will the benefits outweigh the price?

Another sacrifice is family time. Typical students find themselves balancing at least four balls in the air: work, studies, ministry, and family. Both work and studies demand lots of attention. The time clock at work and periodic exams cannot be ignored. Unfortunately the area easiest to ignore is the family. Thus many families suffer silently for years—but not without repercussions that can affect the student's ministry later in life.

Thus, students will have to plan and use their time wisely. They will have to make and keep commitments to their families, which is a part of their training as well. Those with a spouse and family will be on tight schedules and may need to consider taking an occasional lower grade in a course as a tradeoff for time with the family.

3. *Academic emphasis.* A major criticism aimed at Christian schools in general and seminaries in particular is an overemphasis on academics. While it is agreed that schools are academic institutions by nature, some complain that they are too academic and theoretical, that some teachers spend most of their time on campus in a Christian cocoon and are out of touch with the real world, that their theories are based on old academic models that do not relate well to the typical person in today's culture.

Critics claim that when students graduate, they are not well equipped to function and minister to people on a practical basis who live in the real world. Seminarians know Greek, Hebrew, Bible content, theology, and church history, but they do not know how to lead ministries, evangelize lost people, train leaders, disciple believers, and exegete their culture. A primary area of concern is the development of certain basic skills that are vital to ministry: listening, conflict resolution, problem solving, consensus building, meetings management, risk taking, ministry roles clarification, mentoring, vision casting, networking.

In fact a significant number of larger churches in America will not hire seminary graduates right out of school unless they are from their churches. More and more churches are turning to proven lay leaders in the congregation and use them on a part-time basis or place them in key leadership positions. Again the primary complaint is that when students come out of Bible college or seminary, they are too oriented around academics. It takes so long for them to get over seminary that the cost is not worth the return.

Students must realize that schools are academic institutions and will always favor the theoretical. This does not have to be a problem. Students can resist the temptation to take all theoretical courses and supplement their programs with practical selections. Most schools are offering more electives as a part of their curriculum, allowing students greater freedom and more choice in the courses they take.

A number of schools have begun to better balance the academic with the practical. Change is taking place on most campuses across North America. In the future, more adjunct faculties who regularly minister in the community will be used in teaching roles in institutions. In addition, schools are expanding the practical programs, and most seminaries are requiring more field education.

4. *Ministry exposure.* A major disadvantage in most schools is the students' lack of exposure to the very ministries for which they are preparing. This is due to several factors. First, although most schools do require some kind of ministry exposure—Bible colleges have Christian service responsibilities, and seminaries require field education—these exposures often have not been sufficient to provide students with the necessary experience to graduate and assume a ministry position in a local church or parachurch ministry.

The typical student is too busy to invest the time it takes to get significant ministry exposure. Most have to devote a certain amount of time each day to outside employment to make ends meet. The rest of their day is spent pursuing studies and spending some time with their families. Thus little time is left over for quality ministry exposure. The old proverb "You can't get blood out of a turnip" applies to the student's time commitments. And the real tragedy is that this experience can cultivate a bad attitude in some students toward what little bit of ministry exposure they do have.

One other factor is academia is valued more than practical ministry in an academic environment. Every student is in the process of developing a core set of values. While in school, those values take a definite turn in the direction of the theoretical away from the practical. Students begin to believe that while in school it is essential that they stress the academic side of their preparation to the exclusion of the practical. When they graduate, they think there will be time to add the ministry essentials to their portfolio. However, after graduation it is too late to pick up the ministry essentials. Most ministries and churches want people who have academic and ministry credentials along with several years of practical experience.

Consequently many schools are joining forces with other ministry organizations. The future will see more schools partnering with local churches and parachurch ministries in the preparation of students for ministry. Some seminaries, for example, are moving toward splitting their curriculum between the academic and the practical. The school will address the subjects handled best in the classroom, such as languages and church history, while the church or parachurch will address the practical essentials in the context of actual ministry. Several new schools, such as Seminary of the

East located in the Northeast, are located in church facilities and place a major emphasis on the practical requirements of ministry.

5. *Passive involvement.* A fifth disadvantage to classroom-based education is students tend to learn in a passive rather than active context. A primary teaching method used in most educational institutions is the lecture method, where teachers who are experts in a particular discipline stand and lecture while their students sit, listen, and take notes. Although this is an acceptable method, it tends to be overused and puts students in a passive learning environment.

However, most ministries are aggressive, not passive, in nature. Therefore students graduate and enter the ministry world unprepared for what is ahead of them. The longer they have learned in a passive situation, the longer it will take to adjust to an active situation. This results in several years of unproductive ministry as those adjustments are made. Most ministries are not prepared for or patient with this situation and may find another person, leaving the former student frustrated and disillusioned. Schools hope to offset this somewhat by encouraging the faculty to use a broader range of teaching methods and by requiring more active involvement in ministry.

Practical suggestions for classroom-based education. Christians should benefit greatly from pursuing classroom-based education in a school or seminary setting if they keep the following practical suggestions in mind.

1. *The goal of biblical education.* Students need to distinguish between the purpose of a school and the goal of a biblical or theological education. The purpose of Christian schools and theological seminaries varies depending on such factors as the school's biblical emphases, finances, academic emphases, and current trends in Christian education. Some have viewed the purpose of Christian educational institutions as primarily academic—"the intellectual centre of the church's life."[3] Others see it as more practical—to prepare people for pastoral ministry in America's churches. Most schools in the 1990s do not see their primary purpose as "the intellectual centre of the church's life," or to prepare men for the pastorate. Their purpose is much broader and involves providing both men and women with the basic tools for ministry in both the church and parachurch communities, emphasizing more the intellectual but also the practical aspects of this endeavor.

The goal of a biblical-theological education, however, is different. No school can prepare a student for ministry, even though some claim to do so.

The goal is to equip tomorrow's Christian leaders to begin the lifelong process of biblical-theological education. R. Paul Stevens writes:

> Undoubtedly part of the confusion is caused by a failure to distinguish between the goal of theological education and the purpose of the theological college. Theological education is the lifelong process of forming Christian persons into the maturity of Christ and equipping them to serve God's purposes in the church and world. A theological college can only engage a part of that purpose, a truth usually not appreciated by incoming students. In the West the confusion is problematic; overseas it is debilitating confusion as newer churches without an evolved history of theological education try to make their Bible schools and theological colleges perform the whole task of theological education.[4]

Schools must not promise too much—to prepare students for ministry; and students must not expect too much—to leave school prepared for ministry. Instead students should graduate with the basic skills and values in place to commence a lifetime of learning in a practical ministry involvement.

2. *The importance of the faculty.* Perhaps the most important ingredient of any Christian educational institution is the faculty. As the faculty goes, so goes the school. No Christian school will ever rise above the quality of its faculty. All else—the administration, curriculum, facilities—either helps or hinders a good teacher. In short, the faculty of a school sets the pace and establishes the quality of that school.

Therefore students should set a high priority on the quality of a school's faculty in selecting the right school for them. Most schools list their faculty and pertinent information about them in the catalog. You should explore such things as their academic credentials and prior ministry and teaching experience.[5] Also of some importance is the amount of time they have been at the institution and whether or not they have published.

An important quality of any faculty is their attitude toward their students. The proper biblical attitude is that the faculty is present to serve, not lord it over their students (Matt. 20:25–28). It is imperative that they have a servant's heart. But how can you determine a faculty's attitude toward students? Sometimes this can best be determined by visiting a school and meeting with some of its faculty members. If they do not have time to meet with you, then you have your answer. Another approach is to identify and interview some of the school's recent alumni ministering in your area of the country.

3. *The curriculum.* Next in importance to the faculty of a school is its curriculum. In general the curriculum is at the heart of any program you should decide to pursue. Therefore you will need to review the curriculum offerings of the various programs of each school, looking for what best meets your ministry needs. Once you know your personal ministry vision, then you will know in general the best program and curriculum for you.

No perfect curriculum exists in any school. Most schools strive for a balance between their educational, spiritual, and practical goals. In reality, usually one is emphasized more than another—that is human nature. However, this can usually be detected by observing how much of the curriculum is given to each area. For example, a particular school may say that it emphasizes the development of godly character in its students, yet it offers little work or academic credit in this area.

Most schools have various distinctions for which they are noted. That may be a consistent theology or a particular doctrinal stance, a practical or Bible-centered curriculum, a unique faculty, or an emphasis on a particular ministry area such as missions. Often these will be listed at the front of the catalog under the reasons why you should attend the particular institution. Again these distinctions will be reflected mostly by the academic courses that make up the curriculum. Ultimately they are important and will either contribute to or distract from your ministry training.

4. *The relationship to the church or parachurch.* Some schools find themselves in competition with churches and other parachurch organizations. Over the years a gap has developed between these Christian schools, particularly theological seminaries, and certain churches—mostly megachurches that have sprung up over the last decade or two.

The chief complaint of the megachurches is the seminaries in general are not adequately training their students to pursue quality ministry in the twenty-first century church. When the typical student graduates, it takes too long for him or her to get over the academic emphasis to become ministry-effective. Some parachurch ministries have voiced the same complaint and, like many of the megachurches, train their own people. Recently, more seminaries have acknowledged there is some justification for this complaint and are committed to addressing this and similar issues.

The wise student will investigate the school's relationship with the churches and parachurch ministries in the community and beyond. Christian schools need the input of the church and the parachurch, and the latter need the schools. The church and parachurch organizations provide the necessary practical ministry training opportunities that no school can duplicate, while the schools serve to perpetuate among other things the orthodox Christian faith. Students should ask about the opportunities that exist in the community and beyond for practical ministry training. They should inquire as to what educational programs are conducted jointly by the school and other ministry organizations.

Ministry-Based Training

Another important context in preparing for your ministry vision is ministry- or field-based training. This training takes place in either the local church or the various parachurch organizations. In general these groups provide training for those who plan to pursue ministry in their organizations. For example, Christians intensively trained by Campus Crusade for Christ normally pursue some kind of campus ministry.

The advantages of ministry-based education. As with classroom-based education, ministry-based education has certain distinct advantages. Some of the disadvantages of classroom-based education are the advantages of ministry-based education. Three such advantages are low costs, a practical emphasis, and active involvement in the learning process. A fourth is ministry credentials.

1. *Low costs.* Whereas the costs of a college or seminary education have become prohibitive for some, little if any cost is involved in ministry-based education. Local churches do not charge for the training of voluntary workers. In fact the church has an obligation to provide the best training possible for its people if it is to make an impact in its community.

Neither do they charge those who are involved in ministry over a temporary period, such as an internship. The same is true for parachurch ministries. The only situation where cost might be a factor is when a student does an internship from out of the area and has to cover basic living expenses. And in some cases funds are available to cover even these costs. From the financial perspective, ministry-based education excels.

2. *Practical emphasis.* While classroom-based training carries with it an academic emphasis, field-based training carries a practical emphasis. It is ministry intensive. If you have to err in one direction, the practical direction is best. Ultimately the object of the school and the classroom is training for practical ministry. However, practical training should be based on solid academics—what an organization does should have been carefully thought through and be biblically correct.

Field training does run the risk of straying from biblical-theological truth. It continually faces the temptation of doing what it does "because it works," falling into the trap of ministering on a pragmatic as opposed to a biblical basis. That which is pragmatic may not be biblical; whereas, that which is biblical is always pragmatic in some way.

However, just as the school can and must include the practical, so ministry-based training can and must include academics that focus on divine truth. This is the emphasis of new church-based organizations such as BILD International (Biblical Institute of Leadership Development), which attempts to combine solid biblical and theological education in a ministry context.

3. *Active involvement.* While schools often educate students in a passive context, ministries place their people in active learning situations. It is rare in a ministry-based context for trainees to sit and listen to lectures. At worst a trainee is placed in a ministry situation and is expected to perform with little or no preparation. If the ministry happens to be a good fit, the trainee may prosper regardless. A poor fit leads "only" to ministry disaster. At best, the trainee works under a mentor who explains the ministry, demonstrates how to do the ministry, and then critiques the ministry performance.

4. *Ministry credentials.* An advantage that classroom-based and ministry-based training have in common is ministry credentials. Actual ministry experience provides you with the credentials to minister in many organizations.

In the second half of the twentieth century, some ministry organizations, particularly larger churches in mainline denominations, prefer or even require that their professional people have some kind of academic degree (academic credentials). This degree confers on them the right to minister (ministry credentials). In other organizations, in this age of professionalism, an academic degree has given some individuals an advantage over those who would attempt to minister without one.

But at the end of the twentieth century this has begun to change in some quarters due in part to the megachurch phenomenon mentioned above. Consequently either an internship or a staff position in certain ministries grants a believer the necessary ministry credentials. In fact, some detect a growing bias against people with academic degrees, especially from a seminary. In the 1990s a number of larger churches have become dissatisfied with seminary training and have begun to train their own people for their full- and part-time staff positions.

The disadvantages of ministry-based education. While a growing number of pastors believe that ministry-based education is superior to classroom-based, the former does have some disadvantages. The more important ones are personal sacrifices, biblical-theological accuracy, and a limiting ministry model.

1. *Personal sacrifices.* Christians who pursue ministry-based training may not face the same sacrifices as those in classroom-based contexts. Unless they live a significant distance away from where the ministry organization is based, they do not have to move themselves or their families.

However, they have to make other sacrifices. Like classroom-based education, field-based training takes time whether you pursue it part- or full-time. A perennial problem facing most organizations is a lack of staff. Consequently the existing staff and often trainees put in long, intense hours in ministry, which results in limited time with family. Also if the ministry does not provide remuneration, the full-time trainee must either raise support or maintain a part-time job, which absorbs additional time.

2. *Biblical-theological accuracy.* A responsibility that most churches have shared since the beginning of Christianity is the preservation and transferral of the orthodox Christian faith. What the church and parachurch believe (doctrine) is foundational to what they do (praxis). Because most ministries live constantly in the area of the practical, the doctrinal may experience some slippage over time.

Ministries are established to reach people, and they often attract a wide diversity of people with different beliefs. Because every ministry needs finances to survive, the temptation to "fudge" on some doctrinal beliefs is ever present. Also, when a ministry is reaching large numbers of people, many begin to wonder if doctrinal distinctions really matter. Often only a fine line exists in leaders' minds between what in their distinct theology they can give up and what they must cling to.

3. *A limiting ministry model.* Each ministry has its own unique ministry strategy that makes up its ministry model. It takes into consideration such things as where the ministry is located geographically, who makes up its target group, the strengths and weaknesses of its ministry team, and so on. Consequently Christians trained in these ministries will function best within them or others similar to them. A common mistake for some church planters is to train under a particular ministry model and then attempt to implement it in a different context. It simply does not work, and the ministry does not survive. Those trained in a unique ministry must be aware of this and either choose to minister in similar situations or apply the broad ministry knowledge and skills they have acquired in a different situation.

Practical suggestions for ministry-based training. While Christians can benefit from classroom-based education, they must have ministry-based education. In pursuing this, several practical suggestions should prove helpful and result in the best ministry exposure.

1. *Seek a quality ministry organization.* In the pursuit of ministry training, not just any organization will do. Seek out the best opportunity available. In a bad situation, you learn what not to do, but that is not enough. You need a good situation where you can learn what to do and how to do it well.

What should you look for? First, evaluate the ministry's vision and its strategy to implement that vision. Second, try to determine if the ministry is maintenance-oriented (content with the status quo) or ministry-oriented. Third, look for a ministry with a good reputation, remembering, however, that any ministry God is using and blessing will be criticized even by well-meaning Christians, especially if the ministry is trying new paradigms. Fourth, look for a ministry that emphasizes character over programs. Not that programs are unimportant, but godly character is much more important. Leaders with godly character have above all a passion for Christ and care more about their people than their programs. Fifth, determine if the ministry offers the range of opportunities necessary to test your vision.

2. *Seek a ministry organization that fits your vision.* Not only is a quality ministry organization important, but it should closely mirror your vision. If God is directing you to work in a church, then pursue your training in a church—if in a parachurch ministry, then train in a parachurch setting. If you are designed to minister best in a new paradigm context, you will be frustrated in an old paradigm. The same is true for those designed to work in an old paradigm context.

3. *Look for a ministry staff committed to equipping its people for ministry.* The key person is the ministry's leader. If the leader is not committed to equipping people, then the ministry will not be committed to it, and the quality of your training is questionable. Leaders tend to pursue what they do well and ignore or delegate what they do not do well. Do the leaders of the ministry spend any time with trainees? Are they actively involved mentoring people as well as involving their staff in the same?

4. *Agree upon the expectations of the trainer and trainee in advance.* Any ministry situation has expectations. The staff has expectations of its people and its trainees. The people and trainees in turn have expectations of their staff and trainers. For example, a seminary student doing an internship in a large church may expect to preach on Sunday mornings. However, the trainer and senior pastor as well as the church board may not share this expectation. Sunday school teachers or small-group leaders may expect a trainer to observe them and evaluate their ministry or provide them with additional learning resources. Due to a large number of responsibilities, the trainer may not have the time to follow through. If these expectations are not addressed early in the training process, the results are disappointment, disagreement, and hard feelings.

Both parties should address their expectations at the beginning of the relationship. The trainer and trainee should write out all of their expectations, fully discuss them, and adjust where possible. If both parties agree on the final product, they are ready to pursue the training process. Finally, they should write down the adjusted, accepted expectations should any problems or questions arise later.

5. *Design a ministry training plan.* Someone has said, "To fail to plan is to plan to fail." You must insist that a good plan be developed. If your trainer is slack in this area, then you take the lead and design it yourself with the trainer's input. Some ministries have training plans that are too broad or general for adequate training to take place. Such plans are designed for you to fit them; instead you should seek to develop a specific plan that fits you.

Supplementary Training

Supplementary training is not designed to replace or substitute for classroom- or ministry-based training. Instead it serves to work in addition to them.

There are several examples of supplementary training. One is the seminar. A Sunday school teacher can gain valuable insight by attending a Sunday school seminar. A college or seminary student should attend a pastor's conference to gain additional expertise while going through school. Usually seminars take place over a one- or two-day period in a classroom-based context and focus primarily on ministry concerns. Notable examples are the valuable seminars conducted by the Charles E. Fuller Institute of Evangelism and Church Growth.[6] Another is the basic and advanced small group seminars conducted by the Serendipity organization.[7]

A second type of supplementary training is the conference or convention. The only difference from the seminar is they take place over a longer period of time, three to five days on average. For example, there are the well-attended pastor's conferences put on by Saddleback Valley Community Church (Pastor Rick Warren), Grace Community Church (Pastor John McArthur), both in Southern California, and Willow Creek Community Church (Pastor Bill Hybels) near Chicago.

A third type of supplementary training is continuing education. Many schools see the need to provide additional training for their students after graduation, and so they send their faculty to other locations where they spend a day in a classroom context.

A fourth example of supplementary training is the growing number of books, periodicals, and tape ministries available.

The advantages of supplementary training. There are numerous advantages to supplementary training:

- It keeps you up-to-date in your ministry field.
- It may provide training that church, college, or seminary cannot and does not provide.
- It can stimulate creativity and innovation by exposing you to the experiences and thinking of others.
- It is short-term, relaxed, and not ministry intensive.
- It is encouraging to be around others in similar situations, to find you are not alone with your problems.
- You meet people from different theological or philosophical persuasions and may find you have much in common.

- It stimulates change. Some pastors bring their boards to pastor's conferences so they all return "on the same page" in their vision for change.
- It allows you to get away and relax.

The disadvantages of supplementary training. While the disadvantages to this kind of training are few, some do exist. First, it tends not to go far enough. You get good information, but it may not be enough information. It can be only enough information to get you into trouble—you know how to start something but not how to finish it.

Supplementary training can be expensive. Most seminars and conferences charge a fee. There is the cost of food, travel, and accommodations. Books, periodicals, and tapes though valuable can be expensive for most ministry budgets as well. Supplementary training can be discouraging. Those ministering in difficult situations may see little hope for their organizations after attending a conference put on by a highly successful ministry. Or if they attend by themselves, they become discouraged if their people later do not catch the new vision.

There is little time for personal, one-on-one interaction with the seminar or conference presenter since the time is too short or the crowd too big.

So far we have explored two facets of your ministry plan: its concept and contents. Chapter 8 will add the third and fourth facets of the plan. It will help you design a plan tailor-made for your situation and provide several examples of such a plan from the lives of Carol, Tom, and David.

The Development
of a Training Plan

How Do You Design
Your Personal Ministry Plan?

David, Tom, and Carol are excited about how God has "wired" them for ministry, and they are delighted in the direction of their personal ministry visions. Perhaps for the first time, they feel a strong sense of meaning and spiritual purpose. All the missing pieces of the puzzle have fallen into place. As King David did (Acts 13:36), they have a growing desire to serve God's purpose in their generation. As long as they are alive, there will be no sitting on the sidelines for them. They plan to pursue their God-directed ministries with a passion.

They are convinced they need to develop a ministry plan, a road map to move from where they are to where they hope to be in the near future. They have been briefed on the ingredients that go into such a plan, so the only thing left is to answer two key questions: What is the design of the plan? What will it look like when it is finished?

The Design of a Ministry Plan

The design of your personal ministry plan involves both a process and a product. First, you carefully work through a guided process that provides you with the information for the contents of your plan. Then you are ready to produce the product—a written plan—that answers the question, What does this ministry plan look like?

The Design Process

The design process focuses on three areas. They are the three Cs introduced in chapter 7: your life circumstances, your ministry competencies, and your ministry training contexts. These make up a significant portion of your training plan. The design process is an information-gathering phase. The key to the process is to work through the three Cs, asking numerous questions and collecting as much information as is available.

Your Life Circumstances

According to chapter 7 a vital aspect of discovering your divine design is discerning your life situation. With your design and direction in one hand, you need to walk carefully through each of the following circumstances collecting pertinent information with the other hand.

Age. In light of your present age, how should you prepare for your ministry? If you are in your twenties or younger, you have your life ahead of you. If you decide classroom-based ministry is to play a significant part in your plan, then you need to pursue it at this time in your life. Your goal is to have the greatest impact for Christ during the brief time you have on this earth (1 Cor. 9:24–27; Acts 13:36), and there is a decided advantage to pursuing any classroom-based training early. However, avoid the temptation to pursue this training in exclusion to ministry-based training. While it may take a little longer to finish school, you need not be in a hurry.

If you are a lay person, your church will be delighted to use your skills and abilities regardless of how long it takes you to complete the process. If you are preparing for professional ministry such as the pastorate, you will discover that most churches will be more interested in your ministry when you are more seasoned and in your thirties. Use your twenties to complete the majority of your classroom-based training and to get as much ministry-based training as possible. If you plan to pastor, consider a one- or two-year internship at a significant church before diving into the ministry.

If you are in your thirties, you still have a significant portion of your ministry life ahead of you. It is wise to pursue classroom-based education, but do so as soon as possible. It is imperative that you gain ministry-based training because you will enter ministry sooner than if you were in your twenties.

If you are in your forties, fifties, or older, and a lay person, you are approaching a prime time for ministry. You have experienced enough of life to have matured and gained much wisdom. Parachurch ministries and churches will welcome your services with open arms. However, if you are considering beginning a professional ministry, you may not have time for lengthy classroom-based education. Unfortunately many ministries overlook those in their late forties and especially their fifties unless they have already put in a lifetime of significant ministry.

Marital and family status. If you are single and disciplined, you may have more time to invest in preparation for your ministry. If classroom-based training is to be a part of your preparation, try to complete as much of it as possible before you marry. Mixing a heavy work schedule with school is hard on marriages.

However, if you are married, you need to consider several critical factors. First, it is important that your spouse support your ministry plans. Sometimes you can minister as a nonprofessional without spousal support. However, such support is essential to professional ministry. If your spouse is not in favor of it, then ask God to change your spouse's heart. If this does not happen, stay and minister in your present circumstances.

Second, if you have children, you must consider them and their circumstances in your plan. It is easier to pursue school while they are young, as long as you spend time with them. However, if they are in their teens and in high school, you may want to delay any plans to move or attend a school until they have graduated. Moving kids from place to place during adolescence can prove harmful to their emotional and spiritual health.

Third, divorced people will face problems in ministry. This has become less a problem in nonvocational church ministries because a significant number of Christians have experienced a divorce. It may not be a problem for those pursuing a parachurch ministry. However, few churches will consider for the pastorate divorced applicants. In light of the clergy surplus of the 1980s and 1990s, presently it is a buyer's market. If you are divorced and convinced that God wants you to lead a church, then you should consider church planting.

Prior education. The education you have acquired at this time in your life will affect your ministry plan. If you are young and have not completed high school, then you need to do so as soon as possible. A high school diploma or its equivalent is basic to effective ministry in any situation in North America. The question you must consider is, Do you have the basic educational foundation upon which you can build a ministry? The answer to this question directly relates to your plans for any further classroom-based education.

If you have a high school diploma or its equivalent, college may or may not be necessary. Certainly a college education will enhance to some degree any ministry, but there are many situations where you can minister without one. In our day of professionalism, however, a college degree has become almost a necessity if you plan to lead an organization or work on staff with a local church. It grants you a certain degree of credibility.

Gender. Although women have been at the foundation of Christian ministry for centuries, men have dominated the ranks of professional ministry in North America. This has begun to change in the second half of the twentieth century. Most Christian colleges and seminaries make their degree programs available to women on both a master's and doctoral level. Also some evangelical seminaries now have a limited number of women on their faculties. Some evangelical schools will not allow women to pursue pastoral studies. Regardless, a growing number of women in evangelical churches are filling such positions as elder, deacon, worship director, counselor, and director of Christian education.

If you are a woman, you will have professional ministry opportunities in the twenty-first century experienced by few women in the past. Therefore it is imperative that you determine the biblical role of women in ministry. You need to arrive at answers to such questions as, Can I serve as a senior pastor in a church? Does the Bible allow for women elders or deacons? Should women teach men? Whatever your answers to these and other questions like them, you should be ready to defend your position from the Scriptures.

Health and disabilities. A major factor in your ministry plan will always be the health and any disabilities of you and your family. Health involves both the physical and emotional dimensions. Those in good physical health have priority over those in poor health. Vocational and nonvocational ministry often require long hours. This will place a constant strain on you and your family both physically and emotionally. If you are struggling with any serious emotional difficulty, you should not pursue ministry. The top priority on your ministry plan is to get help. But do not give up hope for future ministry. A number of people who have had emotional difficulties have experienced healing and served the Lord professionally, some as excellent lay and professional counselors.

If you have a disability, you will discover that a number of ministries are available to you. The problem is finding a ministry willing to hire a Christian with a disability. In spite of much progress, many Christians still do not understand or are afraid of those with disabilities. The reality is that most will choose a person who is not disabled. Consequently I suggest you consider a ministry with and to people who share your disability. If you are seeing or hearing impaired, serve those who are seeing or hearing impaired. People with various disabilities are often ignored by the average Christian ministry but provide a mission field of activity for those who understand them and have a passion for reaching them.

Finances. Preparation for ministry may or may not prove costly. Most lay people involved in part-time ministry incur few expenses. However, the reverse is true if you desire full-time ministry. Finances play a dominant role if you desire any classroom-based education. You should plan this area carefully. If at all possible, get your education without taking a part-time job. This frees you to pursue both classroom- and ministry-based education. One way to accomplish this is to raise funds to cover your expenses. When you make application to a school, inquire about any available scholarships or grants. Talk to your pastor and friends about possible support.

Your Ministry Competencies

You will recall from chapter 7 that your ministry competencies focus on three areas: your character (being), knowledge base (knowing), and skills (doing). You will need to determine how all of these fit into your lifetime ministry plan because all are necessary for a competent, high-impact ministry.

The development of your character. The development of your character must carry the highest priority. Your ministry is founded on your character. Doing is predicated on being. Failure in character has the potential to ruin forever your ministry. Failure in ministry is much less severe if you have strong, Christlike character. Two areas are critical to your spiritual formation.

The first is the private, individual development of your character. Our Savior has taught us the importance of a quiet time (Mark 1:35). You must set aside a regular time for individual Bible study, prayer, and worship. Both input (Bible study) and output (prayer and worship) are necessary. While we speak to God in our prayers and worship, he speaks to us in his Word (2 Tim. 3:16). And the Savior argues convincingly about our needs in this area: "It is written: 'Man does not live on bread alone, but on every word that comes from the mouth of God'" (Matt. 4:4).

I have two suggestions. First, set aside the best part of your day for your time with God. Some people are at their best early in the morning; others are best at night. Regardless, determine when you are most alert mentally and schedule that time with God. However, some would argue from Christ's example (Mark 1:35) that it is good to begin your day with a quiet time. It sets the mood for the entire day and allows you to put your day in God's hands from the start.

Second, plan to have your devotions in a quiet location where there is little opportunity for interruption. Jesus not only got up early, he left the house where he was staying and went to a solitary place for prayer. Your solitary place may be your bedroom or a study at home, your office or place of work before the day starts, a nearby library, a restaurant, or someplace outdoors.

The other critical but often ignored area is the public, corporate development of your character. A quiet time in itself is not sufficient. We in North America have become a nation of individualists who prefer competing to collaborating. Yet the Scriptures assign high marks for community and collaboration among the saints. We were created for community (Gen. 2:18; 21–22), to serve in community (1 Cor. 12:12–31), and to grow in community (Acts 2:42–47).

I have several suggestions for how you might accomplish your spiritual formation in community. The first is to find someone who will disciple you. Discipleship is the process by which one mature, committed Christian teaches, motivates, prays for, holds accountable, and encourages another disciple to understand and apply biblical principles to his or her life. The primary objective is to develop Christlike character.

The second is to find a spiritual mentor. Discipleship can involve several areas of your life, such as the development of Christlike character, the acquisition of Bible knowledge and theology, involvement in spiritual disciplines, and professional growth in a particular vocational area. Mentoring on the other hand is a subset of discipleship and usually involves focusing on one area of weakness. A mentor is a person who is more mature than you and is willing to help you grow in that particular area.

The first two suggestions raise two important questions. First, Where do you find a discipler or a mentor? And second, What do they look like? The process of finding a discipler or mentor is not as difficult as you might think. Begin with the people in your ministry organization or church, looking for a person with a reputation for walking with the Savior. Ask them if they would be willing to disciple or mentor you. Many mature saints are not involved in these roles simply because no one has pursued them.

A third suggestion regarding your spiritual formation in community is to join a small group. As we approach the twenty-first century, a number of churches have rediscovered the importance of small-group ministries as portrayed in the early church (Acts 2:46; 5:42; 20:20). Small groups provide a private place in which believers can teach, encourage, love, confront, pray for, and give to one another. If your church does not have a vital small-group ministry, perhaps God would have you start one.

The expansion of your knowledge base. Though some have placed too great an emphasis on cognitive learning at the expense of character development and skills acquisition, you must have a knowledge base from which to minister. You must know what you are doing to be competent and credible in ministry. But what do you need to know? Much depends on the nature of your ministry; however, certain basics are imperative for all lay or vocational ministries.

One is a broad knowledge of Scripture and its various doctrines. Surveys of the American public reveal that although nearly half believe the Bible is God's Word, most know little about it—few can even name the four Gospels. I suspect much the same is true of the people in many of America's churches. Effective ministry is based on divine truth found in the Bible. All believers need a working knowledge of the Scriptures to mature in Christ (Heb. 5:11–6:3) and minister effectively (2 Tim. 3:16–17).

I have several suggestions for how you can gain a better knowledge of the Bible. The first is to study it regularly on your own. The Christian bookstore in your community will have a number of resources available to assist you in the process. A second is to invest your life in a local church that believes and teaches the Bible. Such a church usually provides several opportunities to learn the Bible, such as the Saturday or Sunday sermon, Sunday school classes, and small group Bible studies.

Not only do you need to have a general knowledge of the Scriptures, you need to know what it says about certain doctrines. One area is creation. (Where did we come from?) Another is the doctrine of man. (What is our purpose in life?) A third area is the doctrine of sin or evil. (Exactly what is sin and where did it come from? And what are its effects on people?) A fourth is the Savior. (Who is Jesus Christ? What has he done and what difference does he make in our lives?) A fifth is salvation. (How are we saved?) A sixth is the future. (What is God's plan for the future and what is your place in it?) A seventh is the spiritual life. (How do you walk with Christ?) An eighth is the doctrine of angels. (Do angels exist? Is Satan an angel, and if so, what happened to him?)

A second basic area is a knowledge of people, yourself and others. You are more competent in ministry when you understand yourself and others. A key to understanding yourself is knowing and ministering in light of your divine design. A working knowledge of temperament will also help you understand why other people act the way they do. This is an essential for putting together ministry teams.

A third basic area is a knowledge of the ministry essentials, "nuts and bolts," that affect your ministry. These may include preaching, teaching, discipleship, mentoring, leadership, administration, leadership training, counseling, forming strategy, evangelism, lay mobilization, assimilation, dealing with change, baptizing, funerals, weddings, communion. It might seem odd to include such ministry essentials as weddings, funerals, and baptisms as necessary for lay people. Historically these essentials have been reserved for professional clergy. But this is a cultural not a biblical phenomenon. As more churches turn to small-group ministries led by gifted lay people, there is no biblical reason to prohibit them from performing these essentials. This would free up professional clergy for other essentials.

What do you know about biblical leadership? Not only should you know your leadership role (leader or administrator) and your leadership style (autocratic, democratic, participatory, or bureaucratic), you need to understand leadership in general. Also, what do you know about leadership training? Do you know how to select, recruit, and equip leaders for effective ministry?

Whatever God has designed you to do, you need to gain as much information about that area as necessary to function with excellence. If God has designed you to teach a Sunday school class or a men's Bible study, you benefit by knowing as much as possible about the content of your subject and the basic principles of teaching. If you are responsible for the church's sound equipment, you should be up on the latest and best equipment available. If you are a pastor, you should be aware of what God is doing in new ministry paradigms and how they might affect your ministry. One of your responsibilities is to be God's change agent. You are responsible to lead your church through change so that it does not bog down in the status quo and become ineffective in accomplishing the Great Commission.

The acquisition of ministry skills. Competency for ministry also includes the acquisition, reinforcement, and refinement of various critical skills for your ministry. They have a deciding impact on whether and how you accomplish that ministry. The following basic skills are necessary for most ministries and serve as a checklist for your skills development. For each one, determine your present skill level and your goals for future development.

The first is your Bible study skills. How adept are you at studying the Bible? Does the Bible remain a mystery to you? How skilled are you in the areas of observation, interpretation, and application of the biblical text? In what areas are you strong and weak? Do you know where to go for help?

The second is your communication skills, which involves four areas. First is your reading ability. You must determine if you are a good or poor reader. Would you benefit from taking a speed-reading course? How good is your comprehension? Second is your writing skills. Are you effective as a writer or do you struggle? How might writing enhance your ministry? Third is your speaking skills. Are you satisfied with your speaking abilities? How do others respond to your messages or lessons? Are you clear and concise? Fourth is your listening skills. Of the four communication skills, this tends to be the weakest in North America. For example, do you remember people's names when they are introduced to you? In a conversation, do you find your mind tends to wander and you often miss vital bits of important information?

Next on the checklist is your problem-solving skills. Whether you are involved in starting a new ministry or revitalizing an established one, you can count on lots of problems. However, certain temperaments are better at solving these problems than others. Some people enjoy attacking problems and find them a personal challenge.[1] Others view them as obstacles rather than opportunities for ministry. Which category do you fall under? Are you familiar with the principle of integrative problem solving (the idea that the persons who raise problems initially are often the best qualified to find and implement solutions to those problems)? Scripture presents numerous ministry problems. In fact, the Book of Acts is replete with problems. It seems the church was hardly born before it faced one problem after another. The issue is not that they had problems but how they solved their problems. For example, in Acts 6 the twelve apostles faced a problem with the Grecian Jews who complained that their widows were mistreated by the Hebraic Jews. The apostles wisely dealt with the problem by appointing seven godly Grecian Jews (integrative problem solving) to resolve the situation.

The fourth is your conflict resolution skills. This is an aspect of your problem-solving skills that specifically deals with people problems. Research indicates you have a particular style for resolving conflict: avoiding, collaborating, compromising, and competing.[2] You need to discover your unique style and how to most effectively use it.

The fifth is consensus building skills. It is naive in working with groups and committees to believe that all will agree on any topic. Just ask any experienced pastor or board chairman. Consequently a key to effective teamwork and decision making is the consensus method. A consensus is reached when all the members of a group decide to support its decision whether or not all agree. When the meeting is adjourned, everyone supports the outcome. Are you a consensus builder? Do you know how to work with a group and bring about a consensus without a compromise?

The sixth is roles clarification skills. A critical element in a team context is the ability to separate the jobs or tasks of team members from their roles. Often each member has a function spelled out in a job description. However, their role goes beyond a job description to the expectations of a particular team member about his or her job and to the expectations other members have about that same job. This affects task interdependence and ultimately the ability of the group to work together as a team. Are you aware of the importance of roles clarification? Are you skilled in helping a team to clarify the expectations that the various members have of one another as well as of themselves?

The seventh is team building skills. Since New Testament ministry is team ministry, most Christian organizations accomplish more for the Savior if their people function in a team context. However, it is much easier to talk about ministering in a team than to accomplish it. All Christians are not cut from the same bolt of cloth. That they are believers does not mean they all think alike. It takes skill to blend a group of Christians together into an effective team that accomplishes the vision of the ministry organization. Do you know what skills are necessary to achieve this? Do you possess these skills?

There are other important skills vital to ministry. Some are planning and goal setting, managing meetings, risk-taking, monitoring and evaluation, dealing with ineffective people, rewards and recognition, vision casting, meeting and greeting skills, and networking.[3]

Your Ministry Training Contexts

The ministry design process also focuses on the training contexts of your vision. *Training contexts* refer specifically to classroom-based, ministry-based, or supplementary training as discussed in chapter 7. In light of your design and vision, you should examine and ask questions of each training context. You will need to determine if any or all of these are necessary preparation for your ministry direction.

Classroom-based training. The first step is to ask the question, Does my ministry vision require classroom-based education? If your initial answer is no, would this training prove helpful or could it enhance your ministry? If your answer is still no, then you are ready to move to the next training area. Of the three requirements, this one is the most optional.

Should your answer to any of these questions be yes, then the second step is to rate this area in terms of its priority using the categories of high, medium, or low. If classroom-based training is a must, then rate it as high. If it is important but not a must, rate it as medium. If it is not necessary but might enhance your ministry, rate it as low.

The third step is to think through where and how you will obtain classroom-based training. The location of the school could be a factor. As you begin this step, be alert to the institutions that are the closest to your area. You will need information from various schools about their programs designed to equip people for your ministry vision. Interview those involved in your ministry vision or one comparable to it. Ask where they went to school. Seek their advice regarding the programs that would best equip you. Ask, "If you were to do it all over again, what program would you follow?" In addition, write the schools and request a catalog, which will supply such information as the institution's distinctives, entrance requirements, costs, programs, curriculum, faculty, and resources.

Ministry-based training. There is never any question about whether you need ministry-based training. The answer is always yes. Ministry-based training is essential to any ministry, and it must not be overlooked in the design of your ministry plan. In the past, ministry organizations were quick to look for an academic degree on a candidate's resume. Now, at a time when academic degrees are plentiful, these same organizations are looking closely at a candidate's ministry experience, asking, Does the candidate have any experience? What kind of experience? Where did it take place? Ministry-based experience in a well-known, reputable church or parachurch organization often distinguishes applicants on their resumes.

Rate ministry-based training according to its priority. In most cases, it will be marked as high or medium. A possible exception is the believer who has picked up abundant ministry experience in the past. In this situation the individual may be at a point where classroom-based education is a priority. This applies most often to those who have grown up in and been active in a local church or to those who have worked with a parachurch organization such as the Navigators or Campus Crusade for Christ. They have excellent ministry experience but desire more work in Bible and theology.

Determine how and where you will find ministry-based training. The most natural approach is to contact the ministries that serve in the area of your vision. If your vision is to serve your church as a volunteer counselor, then locate someone serving well in this capacity either in your church or another church. If you have a passion for the unborn, then look to the pro-life ministries in your community.

Two problems are evident in this step, especially for those preparing for vocational ministry. In the 1990s a substantial number of church and parachurch organizations have either plateaued or are in decline, making it difficult to locate a strong ministry site. Be prepared to move to another community if necessary. In addition, once you have located a significant ministry organization, they may not have a training position available. Most are inundated with requests and have filled all available positions. Be prepared to put your name on a waiting list. Whatever happens, hang tough and do not give up.

Supplementary training. The first step is to ask the question, Do I need supplementary training? Most believe the answer is yes. Whether you pursue classroom-based or ministry-based training, your ministry development will require a lifetime of preparation. Thus supplementary training will take place along with and after the first two forms. Most often, it is this kind of training that keeps you current.

The second step is to rate it in terms of its priority in your plan. In most cases it will rate from high to medium.

The third step is to be aware of what supplementary training is available and where. While books and periodicals are available anywhere, seminars and conferences are not. Those who plan these events place them in larger urban areas. You may need to do some traveling. Fortunately most colleges and seminaries are located in large urban centers where these events are scheduled. Therefore wise students will anticipate and schedule them on their training plan.

The Design Product

The design product asks, What does the ministry plan look like? You have concluded gathering information in the design process phase and are ready to use it to write out your ministry plan—the final product. You may be tempted to skip this step, especially if you favor a verbal approach over a written one. However, writing out your plan helps you think through and articulate it in a way that is not possible if you only verbalize it. You will select one of two possible formats: the short answer format or the prose format.

The short answer format may best fit your style. It is for those who do not like to write and involves composing short, precise answers to the questions *who, what, where, when,* and *how.* The question *who* draws heavily from your life circumstances and considers the people primarily involved in your ministry plan, such as your family and relatives. The question *what* includes a brief summary of your design and vision followed by your competencies for ministry (character, knowledge, and skills) as determined above in the design process. The question *where* focuses on your training contexts (classroom-based, ministry-based, or supplementary), also determined above in the design process. The question *when* introduces the time factor, asking you to plan when you will begin the development process and includes any other pertinent time factors. The question *how* focuses primarily on finances, asking how you plan to cover any costs involved in your ministry plan.

The term *prose* describes the common, ordinary language found in speaking or writing in contrast to other language forms such as poetry. I use it here to describe the approach favored by those who enjoy writing in depth. Rather than write brief answers to the five questions, it allows you to write extensively on each and include any other factors important to your plan. You may compose as little as a page or as much as ten pages. You have the freedom to pen as much as you desire and include as many details as you wish.

At this point you should have a good idea about the process of developing a ministry plan and what goes into the final product. However, several sample plans will serve to clarify these even further. What would Carol's, Tom's, and David's plan look like first in the short answer format and then in the prose format?

The Short Answer Format

If we applied the short answer format to Carol's circumstances, it would look like this:

1. *Who:* I am a thirty-two-year-old practicing attorney. I am married to my childhood sweetheart, and we have no children. We are in excellent health. Both of his parents are alive and self-supporting. My mom is a widow and occasionally dependent on some financial help.

2. *What:* My divine design includes the spiritual gifts of leadership, mercy, and pastor. I have a passion for shepherding women. My temperament is high I with a secondary D, and my Myers-Briggs score is ENTJ. My ministry vision is twofold: to direct as a lay person the church's small-group ministry program and to lead my own small group of women in the church.

To develop my character I have a quiet time every other day and have invested heavily in my small-group ministry, which meets once a week. To broaden my knowledge base I study my Bible regularly during my quiet time and with my husband before we go to bed at night. I am beginning to understand people better through my work with small groups and my training for this ministry. I confess I need a better working knowledge of certain ministry essentials such as counseling and the small-group process. I hope to gain this in time by taking a course offered at the local community college. To enhance my skills I have taken a skills inventory offered by my pastor. I know where I am weak and where I am strong. In particular I need to work on my skills in the areas of conflict resolution and team building.

3. *Where:* I have decided that any classroom-based training is a low priority at this time. What I really need is some ministry-based training in overseeing a small-group program and in leading a small group. So ministry-based training is a very high priority. I have also given high priority to supplementary training because there is an excellent seminar available on the small-group process as well as several books and periodicals on conflict resolution and team building.

I have a confession. Sometimes I wonder if anyone in the church will be upset that I—a woman—am directing this program!

4. *When:* The church desires to get the small-group program in place as soon as possible, so I've begun to work on it already. I have carved out some time to visit several churches in our community that have recently implemented small-group programs. I have already begun to meet with a small group comprised of women from my church and neighborhood.

5. *How:* The church has set aside a small amount of funds to help me cover some expenses. However, I am willing to spend money out of my own pocket to get this program up and running.

The short answer format applied to Tom's situation could look like this:

1. *Who:* I am a twenty-six-year-old recent graduate from college. Considering my blue-collar background, graduation has been the major accomplishment in my life next to accepting Christ. I am not married, but I am looking. And since I come from a large family with several brothers and sisters, I want to have lots of kids some day. My dad is about to retire due

to ill health. He presently owns and operates a gas station in our rural community back home. He and Mom have saved some money for retirement over the last few years, so they should be okay without my help.

2. *What:* My divine design consists of the spiritual gifts of leadership, administration, evangelism, faith, and teaching. My passion is for unchurched, lost people and Christians who are spiritually "treading water." My temperament is high D with a secondary I, and my score on the Myers-Briggs is ENFP. My ministry vision is to spend the rest of my life pastoring the same church, either in a church planting or a renewal context.

To develop my character I attempt a daily quiet time. I will also be involved in a spiritual formation group required of all seminary students for three semesters. After that I plan to enter an accountability relationship with another seminarian in which we will encourage one another to Christlikeness and hold one another accountable for our spiritual goals. To expand my knowledge base, especially in the Bible, I am depending primarily on seminary and the classes I am required to take, along with the teaching in my church. I also hope to learn much about ministry essentials from my pastor over the next few years. To acquire and enhance my ministry skills, again I am depending on seminary and training for ministry in the church.

3. *Where:* Because I have been a Christian for only a short time, classroom-based training is a high priority. So I plan to enroll in seminary this fall. I have two years of evangelism and discipleship experience with Campus Crusade. However, I will make it a high priority to invest my life in a good church while at seminary and during the summers because I desperately need to get some ministry-based experience in the local church. I also plan to take several seminars on church planting and leadership that will be offered in the community while I am at seminary. I have already read several books on pastoral leadership and church growth, and I subscribe to *Leadership Journal.*

4. *When:* I start seminary in the fall. I have also located an excellent church in the area where I will lead a group of laymen in evangelism and discipleship during the first year. The pastor indicated that if things go well, I might be able to do an internship with him during the summer months.

Regardless, he plans to help me with the various ministry essentials and my skills development. Also I have registered for a seminar in October on preaching to the unchurched.

5. *How:* I have raised enough support to cover my first year at seminary. Several Crusade staff members taught me how to raise funds and helped me in the process. Some college friends have also indicated a desire to help after they are established in their careers. My desire is to raise enough funds to cover all my expenses so that I can devote all my time to seminary and the church (and to looking for a wife!).

Finally, the short answer format for David could look like this:

1. *Who:* I am twenty-eight years old and the recent pastor of a small church in a sleepy little town located in the suburbs of a midsized city. I am married, and my wife and I have chosen not to have any children until I have finished all my schooling. We have recently returned to seminary for more training. She is solidly behind my desire to serve the Lord, and she is willing to work until I finish a doctoral program.

2. *What:* My design consists of the spiritual gifts of administration, teaching, and possibly preaching. I have a passion for teaching the Bible to people who are deeply interested in its truths and desire to explore them in depth. My temperament is high C with a secondary D, and the Myers-Briggs indicated I am an ISTJ. Until recently I thought I was to be a pastor. However, in light of my assessment I now believe I should pursue a teaching ministry on a college or seminary level. I plan to teach in a school on the mission field because there are few teaching positions available in North America.

To develop my character I am good about having a quiet time every day. I am also in a mentor relationship with one of my professors, and we are studying the life of Christ. To expand my knowledge base I continue to study the Bible on my own to supplement my doctoral studies in the department of Bible exposition. Where I need more work is in knowing and understanding people. I have already enrolled in temperament training that will qualify me to administer the Biblical and Personal Profiles to people. I also sense that I need more knowledge of certain ministry essentials such as the training of leaders. They never taught me how to do this in seminary. Finally, due to my limited ministry experience I believe I am weak in many of the skills critical to ministry, especially to the ministry of a teacher. I hope to develop these while in the doctoral program.

3. *Where:* With a personal vision focused on a teaching ministry, classroom-based training is a very high priority. I will need a doctorate to teach in most institutions overseas, and I would like to take some education courses that will orient me to the world of education in general and help me with the art of teaching in particular. A missionary friend suggested that once I know the country where I will teach, I should begin language studies. I have also placed a medium to high priority on ministry-based training. While I now have two years of ministry experience in the pastorate, I do not have any ministry-based experience teaching in the classroom. I hope to get this kind of experience while pursuing my doctorate. Finally I place a lower priority on supplementary training. However, I do plan to attend some meetings (the Evangelical Theological Society and the Society for Biblical Literature) sponsored by some organizations in my academic field as well as read a number of books and articles in periodicals.

4. *When:* My wife and I are presently living in seminary housing, and I have just begun to work on my doctorate, which should take four years to complete. I am currently in the process of writing and interviewing with several mission boards and representatives who sponsor colleges and seminaries in other countries. I hope to have this nailed down by the end of this year or the middle of my second year of studies, so we can begin our language preparation. I plan to finish all my classroom work by the end of my third year and complete the dissertation in time to graduate by the end of the fourth year. I have allowed two years to raise support, so I hope to be on the field in six years.

5. *How:* The company where my wife worked during my prior seminary studies has hired her back with a substantial increase in salary. Both sets of parents are committed Christians, and they are supporting us as well. With my wife's job and the additional parental support we should be able to meet all our expenses for the next four years.

The Prose Format

If Carol had opted for the prose format, it would have looked something like this:

I am thirty-two years old and have been practicing law for the last two years. I enjoy the legal profession and believe it is where I can best serve the Lord. Being an attorney is not easy work, but it gives me the freedom to take some time off to pursue what I believe will be a significant ministry at the church. I married Bob shortly after we both graduated from high school. Presently we have no children. We have tried to have a family, but the doctors say we both have an infertility problem. Otherwise we are in excellent health. For now we have given up on children; perhaps someday we will adopt.

Bob and I both have parents who are living. Bob's dad is nearing retirement from an engineering company in south Texas, and his mother has always been a homemaker. Because of his dad's retirement income and benefits, they will both live comfortably. My father died several years ago and left my mom with just enough income to meet her basic living expenses. Consequently Bob and I and my brother try to help her financially from time to time. Neither of our parents, however, pose any problems for my ministry plans.

I am delighted with how God has designed me. He has blessed me with the gifts of leadership, mercy, and pastor. I have a passion to work with women, especially those who need someone to listen to them and show them care and concern. My temperament is high I and a secondary D, and according to the Myers-Briggs I am an ENTJ. My leadership role is a leader-manager, and my style is a combination of democratic and autocratic. My evangelistic style is relational although at times I may confront a lost person. I am not completely sure of all my natural gifts. I do have a talent for art, which comes from my dad, but I have not sought to develop it to any degree. Lay consultant Bruce Smith suggested that in time I should think about how this could be used for the Lord.

In light of my design and with Bruce Smith's help, I have determined that my personal ministry vision is to lead the church's small-group ministry program and lead a small group consisting mostly of women in the church and a few lost women in my neighborhood. If I think about this ministry at night before I go to bed, I get so excited I cannot fall asleep. In time I may have to give up the leadership of the small-group program. The church is growing rapidly, and eventually it will need to bring in a full-time person to direct the ministry. At that time I will either move to direct another program or assist the new director. I enjoy the shepherding of the women in my small group. They have so many spiritual and emotional problems, and the women from my neighborhood are not yet Christians. They look to me for my leadership and personal counsel—in fact the group is growing.

I am convinced the development of my character is essential to any ministry I pursue in the church. Thus I make sure I have a quiet time every other day, in spite of my busy schedule. My small group has also served to enhance my character development. They constantly pray for and encourage me and have on a few occasions confronted me over certain spiritual glitches in my life. I do not know how I survived spiritually without them.

I desperately need a better knowledge of the Scriptures, so I study them during my quiet time, but I learn the most when my husband and I study the Bible together in the evenings. We both have a voracious appetite for the Scriptures and study them as much as possible. We also soak in the Bible teaching at our church. I am gaining a better understanding of people through my training for the small-group ministry—I am studying the various temperaments and how they relate to one another. I need work in some of the ministry essentials for my unique ministry. In particular I need more knowledge about counseling and the small-group process. I have found a book on each topic at the public library, and I plan to work through the exercises at the back of each book over the next month. Also I plan to take some courses in these areas offered at the local community college in the next year.

I am also convinced of the importance of developing skills for my ministry. I have taken a skills inventory and know that I need to develop skills in the areas of conflict resolution and team building. I scored low in these two areas and realize their importance to my ministry. I am not sure yet how I will accomplish this.

Much of my professional training has taken place in both an undergraduate and graduate context. My degrees are in American history and law; thus I have experienced a lot of classroom-based learning over the past few years. While I am open to more of this kind of training, I do not see it as a high priority for my ministry vision. In time I may take a class or two as mentioned above at a nearby community college. For now I place high priority on ministry-based and supplementary training. I have scheduled meetings with some lay and professional directors of small-group programs at churches in the area. My plan is to learn as much as I can from them. And if I can find the time, I may try to gain some expertise working with the programs in their churches. In two months I will attend the Serendipity small-group seminar that will be conducted in our town. I have also subscribed to a magazine that focuses on small-group ministries and have purchased several books on the same.

I am told some people in the church believe that women should not be in any leadership roles. I wonder how they will feel about my position as the leader of the small-group program? I have read most of the biblical texts on the subject of the woman's role in ministry, and I do not see any problems with what I am doing. I also have the full support of the pastoral staff and the church board.

When I asked the pastor how soon he wanted the small-group ministry up and running, he replied, "Yesterday!" So I dropped several minor projects and have been working on the program ever since. While several small groups have already formed on their own, I hope to have the formal program in place in less than a year.

The pastor and board are behind this nonbudgeted ministry to the extent that they have given money from their own pockets. Presently I have $2,000 to work with. For now this amount should be sufficient to cover my travel costs, the seminar, and the books and magazines. Regardless, I so believe in what I am doing that I will gladly take money out of my own pocket to implement the program.

If Tom had chosen the prose format, it might have resembled the following longer plan:

I am twenty-six years old and could have graduated from college at twenty-three, but I had to work a couple of years at my dad's gas station to save up enough money to go to school. We are what some call a blue-collar family, and I am the first one in my family to graduate from college, which I consider a major accomplishment. My dad has worked most of his life in a local gas station. He began as a young boy pumping gas. Eventually he learned how to be a mechanic. Finally he was able to save enough money to purchase the station when it came up for sale. He has worked hard all his life but never had enough money to send any of his five kids to college. He and Mom are proud that I have a college degree even though they never emphasized school when we were growing up. He is about to retire due to a mild heart attack and rheumatoid arthritis. He wants his college-graduate son to take over the operation of the station, but he has accepted the fact that my oldest brother will have to do that.

I am fascinated with how God has designed me. He has chosen to give me the spiritual gifts of leadership, administration, evangelism, faith, and teaching. I have a passion to reach out to and spend time with unchurched, lost people. I also have a passion to help Christians who seem to be "stuck in neutral" in their spiritual growth. My temperament is high D and secondary I, and I am an ENFP on the Myers-Briggs Inventory. My leadership role is a leader-manager and my style is a combination of autocratic and democratic. After two years of heavy evangelistic ministry with Campus Crusade, it is obvious to everyone that my evangelistic style is confrontational. I even walked up to the college president one day and to everyone's surprise spoke with him about his salvation. I think I have a natural gift for leadership; I play the guitar, and some people tell me I sing well, although I have had no formal training in music or voice.

Several Crusade staff members and the ministry consultant who taught our dorm Bible studies agree that my personal ministry vision is to pastor a new paradigm, cutting-edge church with a Great Commission vision. They had hoped I would come on staff with Crusade but realized that God was directing me away from parachurch to local church ministry. I find the thought of leading and pastoring a church exciting, though I am not sure yet whether I should go into church planting or church renewal. Since I see the need for and prefer new paradigm ministries, I suspect I may be a church planter. Also, my gift and experience in evangelism are well suited for church planting.

I know all too well the importance of developing my character. Campus Crusade did an excellent job of driving this into my thick skull. Consequently I attempt to have a quiet time every day. I say "attempt" because I do miss once or twice a week when I get real busy. In addition to my quiet time, the seminary requires that all seminary students involve themselves in spiritual formation groups for three semesters. These groups will help me focus on my depravity in the context of my dignity as a Christian. When

I finish the spiritual formation requirements, I hope to become a leader of a group the last year. I also plan to form an accountability relationship with another seminary student. We will meet once a week and hold each other accountable for our walk with Christ and the accomplishment of the spiritual goals we set for ourselves each month.

I need to expand my knowledge of the Bible and doctrine. In fact that is one reason why I have enrolled in seminary. Though I have been involved in parachurch ministry and have studied the Bible, I want to work systematically through the Scriptures and theology with professors who are thoroughly trained in their areas of expertise. If the seminary curriculum delivers on its promises, I should accomplish this goal. Due to my parachurch training, I have found I have a good knowledge of many of the ministry essentials. I hope to gain some help in ministry essentials that relate specifically to the local church from a pastor or someone in the church I attend while in seminary. In particular I see a need to know more about church planting and church renewal. The seminary offers electives in these two areas that should give me the essential knowledge base critical to my future.

What I have said about my knowledge of the ministry essentials also applies to my ministry skills. The more I work on my ministry plan, the more I appreciate my parachurch ministry experience. I am amazed at the skills I have developed while working with Crusade on the college campus as a student. I feel strong in my communication, problem-solving, and conflict-resolution skills. My goal is to discover where I am weak in the skills necessary to pastor a church. I hope to get help with these in the church I attend while in seminary.

My professional training has taken place in college on an undergraduate level in the school of business. My degree is in business administration. Though I have completed four years of classroom-based training, I have only been saved for two years and need more training in Bible, theology, and church history. Thus I place a high priority on classroom-based education. I have already decided to pursue either the church planting or church renewal tracks in the pastoral ministries department at seminary.

I place high priority on ministry-based training as well as classroom-based. I have met the pastor in an excellent church not far from the seminary who has agreed to allow me to lead a group of laymen in the areas of evangelism and discipleship and indicates that he might be available to mentor me through several summer internships. He is also interested in using his church to plant a daughter church in the next county in two or three years. Perhaps I will play a significant role in birthing that new church.

I also value supplementary training. I have discovered that the Charles E. Fuller Institute of Evangelism and Church Growth will conduct two weekend seminars in the city, one during the fall and the other during the spring semester. I have already mailed in the tuition for the seminar on leadership to take advantage of their "early bird" special. In addition to reading books on pastoral ministry, leadership, and church growth, I have a four-year subscription to *Leadership Journal*—a graduation gift from my sister.

For a while I debated whether I should try to work my way through seminary to cover my expenses. Then several of the Crusade staff took me aside and taught me how to raise funds. They said I was a natural. In a period of six months I raised enough money to cover one year of expenses while at seminary. A significant portion came from several people whom I won to Christ and then discipled. Others have indicated a desire to involve themselves financially with me when they become more established in the marketplace. My parents said they wanted to help, but Dad's retirement will not allow it.

Finally I suspect that David, who likes to write, will opt for the prose format. His plan will look something like this:

I am twenty-eight years old and have just completed two years in the pastorate of a small church that proved to be a disaster. They were the most frustrating years of my life. Had it not been for my wonderful wife, I might not have survived as well as I have. I am convinced that God used these two years to show me that I am not cut out to be a pastor, as our parents once thought. He also used this opportunity to provide me with valuable ministry experience and insight.

Obviously I am married. In fact, we just celebrated our fourth anniversary. We have chosen not to begin a family until I complete my doctoral studies. This will prove hard on my wife since she is from a large family and loves kids. But we both agree that I should be in school, and she is fully committed to work and support us until I finish.

God has blessed us with two wonderful sets of parents. Both fathers are pastors who love the Lord and are serving him in their churches. My mom works while my wife's mom is a homemaker. They pray for us regularly and have always given us wise counsel—except when they advised me to become a pastor. I think both were blinded by their desire to see someone else in the family, a son or at least a son-in-law, become a minister.

I am amazed how God has designed me. I only wish I had discovered it earlier in life. He has given me the spiritual gifts of administration, teaching, and possibly a cross-cultural gift of some sort (I am fascinated with people from other cultures). Of the three, teaching is my strong suit and is at the center of my gift-cluster. While my last congregation questioned my people skills, many times they complimented me on my ministry of teaching—they learned a lot of Bible over the last two years. I believe one reason for this is my passion for teaching the Bible to those who want to probe deeply into its spiritual truths. My temperament, according to the Biblical Personal Profile, is high C with a secondary D. The Myers-Briggs indicates I am ISTJ. My leadership role is manager, and my style is bureaucratic. I must confess I am weak in the area of evangelism, but I think my style is intellectual. I have several natural gifts, such as acting, speaking, cooking, and auto mechanics, that could serve me well on the mission field.

My personal vision is to pursue teaching on a college or seminary level with a mission organization in a foreign culture. Most missions organizations prefer a doctorate for those who teach in their schools. This gives the organization more credibility in the eyes of foreign governments. Consequently I place a high priority on classroom-based education. I would also like to pursue studies in the field of education. I am not really aware of what takes place in an educational institution, and I need to take some courses in the methodology of teaching. With my gift of administration I plan also to take one or two courses in educational administration. Most likely, God will use me in an administrative position in addition to teaching. A missionary friend suggested that once I know the country where I will minister, I should begin formal or informal language preparation. This is excellent advice.

I realize now the importance of developing my character. I say "now" because while I was in seminary everybody talked about it, but not many students were doing something about it. There were no spiritual formation groups when I went through seminary, and I failed to see the importance of a regular quiet time with God. Instead I managed to convince myself that I could accomplish spiritual formation by doing my homework devotionally. It did not work, and I paid dearly for it in the first year of my pastorate. Now I take advantage of my obsessive-compulsiveness, and I rarely miss my daily quiet time, even on holidays! I have also developed a close friendship with one of my profs. We meet once a week for lunch and are presently studying the life of Christ together with an emphasis on applying the truths to our lives.

I have a good knowledge base in the Scriptures (my problem, like so many, is applying the truths to my life). I majored in Bible exposition in seminary, and I am working on my doctorate in the same area. I continue to expand my knowledge through personal study and through my doctoral courses. After two rough years in the ministry, I have discovered I need a better knowledge of people. I really don't understand why people do some of the things they do. I plan to take the professional training that prepares people to administer both the Personal and the Biblical Profile. This will thoroughly orient me to the four temperaments. I have also agreed to listen more carefully to my wife, who understands people well.

My ministry experience also showed me that I am weak in my knowledge of some ministry essentials and critical ministry skills. I do not know how to train leaders, and I do not know enough about leadership, as they hardly touched on these issues in my seminary training. Due to my limited ministry experience (somehow I got out of my internship in seminary), I have not adequately developed the skills important to ministry. I plan to get some of this in my church. This inadequacy applies specifically to teaching. I hope this information is covered somewhere in the doctoral program. While the program does not require any classwork in teaching or education (which seems strange), I plan to take a teaching internship under my professor friend.

For a while I placed a low priority on ministry-based education. I thought I only needed it for the pastorate or some other practical ministry. However, having observed a number of excellent teachers at the seminary, I am convinced I would benefit from an internship with one of them. After all, the best way to learn to teach is to teach. As already mentioned, I have asked one professor, and he has consented to work with me. Along with this opportunity, we are attending and ministering in a Hispanic church to gain exposure to people of another culture. This is for my wife's benefit as well as my own. She is open to the mission field but wants and needs more exposure to cross-cultural contexts.

I rate supplementary training a low to medium priority. There aren't many seminars for teachers and professors. However, there are a few, as well as some professional organizations that hold annual meetings, such as the Evangelical Theological Society and the Society of Biblical Literature. If I can afford it, I would love to travel to Israel for several weeks of study. For now this is only a dream.

I plan to finish my studies and assume a teaching position on the mission field in six years. Normally the doctorate takes four years to complete, which includes three years of classroom preparation and one year to research and write the dissertation. I hope to select and be accepted by an appropriate mission agency at the end of my second year. My wife and I also plan to determine our country for ministry and begin to learn its language and culture by the end of the third year. My personal goal is to have a working knowledge of the language by graduation.

During the last two years we will travel to various churches and meet with people to raise our support. I know the value of networking and plan to meet a lot of Christian people over the next four years both in and beyond the seminary community. Some have already expressed an interest in our future, specifically our parents' churches. I am presently making a list of people we have ministered to or recently met who might become involved in our support. We have committed this timetable to the Lord and believe he will direct us according to his marvelous sovereign will (James 4:13–15).

My wife has agreed to work for the next four years as our primary means of support. As soon as her old boss heard she was coming back to town, he called and offered to increase her salary and benefits significantly. When we arrived in town, he took us to a fashionable restaurant and confessed he did not realize her value to the company until she was gone. She was delighted and agreed to return to work.

Another source of income is our parents. They supported us during our prior time in seminary and want to do so again. In fact their churches, which have served as our home churches, recently agreed to support a limited number of students involved in ministry preparation. They (along with most churches in North America) have never done this before. I suspect that pressure from our parents and those of other students preparing for ministry had a lot to do with the change of heart.

Designing Your Personal Ministry Plan

1. What are your life circumstances?

    a. Age:

    b. Marital and family status:

    c. Prior education:

    d. Gender:

    e. Health and disabilities:

    f. Finances:

    g. Other:

2. Briefly jot down the main ingredients of your divine design.

    a. Spiritual gifts:

    b. Passion:

    c. Temperament:

    d. Leadership role and style:

    e. Evangelism style:

    f. Natural talents and gifts:

3. What is your personal ministry vision?

4. For the sake of your competence for ministry, what are you doing to grow and develop in the following areas?

   a. Your character:

   b. Your knowledge base (Bible, people, ministry essentials, and other areas):

   c. Your ministry skills:

5. What are the training contexts for your vision?

   a. Classroom-based training

      A requirement?

      Priority?
        High ___
        Medium___
        Low___

      Where and how?

   b. Ministry-based training

      A requirement?

      Priority?
        High___
        Medium___
        Low___

      Where and how?

   c. Supplementary training

      A requirement?

Priority?
    High___
    Medium___
    Low___

Where and how?

6. In light of the information above, write out your ministry plan using either the short answer format or the prose format. Be sure to consider the following:

a. *Who* is involved in your plan (spouse, children, relatives)?

b. *What* is involved in your plan (design, vision, and competencies)?

c. *Where* will you realize this plan (contexts)?

d. *When* do you hope to implement this plan (timing)?

e. *How* will you implement this plan (finances)?

Appendix *A*

Spiritual Gifts Inventory

Instructions for Responding

1. Work through each of the following 110 statements on spiritual gifts. After each, check the appropriate box that best describes to what extent the statement accurately describes you.

2. Do not answer on the basis of what you wish was true or what another says might be true, but on the basis of what to the best of your knowledge is true of you.

Questions

	Never	Rarely	Sometimes	Often	Always
	1	2	3	4	5
1. I enjoy working with others in determining ministry goals and objectives.			☒		
2. I have a strong desire to start or be involved in a new ministry.			☒		
3. I delight in telling lost people about what Christ has done for them.		☒			
4. It bothers me that some people are hurting and discouraged.				☒	

	Never	Rarely	Sometimes	Often	Always
	1	2	3	4	5
5. I have a strong ability to see what needs to be done and believe that God will do it.	☐	☐	☐	☒	☐
6. I love to give a significant proportion of my resources to God's work.	☐	☐	☐	☐	☒
7. I have a strong capacity to recognize practical needs and to do something about them.	☐	☐	☐	☐	☐
8. I have a clear vision for the direction of a ministry.	☐	☐	☐	☐	☐
9. I always feel strong compassion for those in difficult situations.	☐	☐	☐	☐	☐
10. I have a strong desire to nurture God's people.	☐	☐	☐	☐	☐
11. I spend a significant portion of my time each week studying the Bible.	☐	☐	☐	☐	☐
12. I am motivated to design plans to accomplish ministry goals.	☐	☐	☐	☐	☐
13. I prefer to create my own ministry problems than to inherit others.	☐	☐	☐	☐	☐
14. I have a strong attraction to lost people.	☐	☐	☐	☐	☐
15. I am very concerned that more people are not serving the Lord.	☐	☐	☐	☐	☐
16. I have a strong capacity to trust God for the difficult things in life.	☐	☐	☐	☐	☐
17. I am eager to financially support ministries that are accomplishing significant things for God.	☐	☐	☐	☐	☐
18. I enjoy helping people meet their practical needs.	☐	☐	☐	☐	☐
19. I find that I have a strong capacity to attract followers in my ministry.	☐	☐	☐	☐	☐
20. I am always motivated to sympathize with those in the midst of a crisis.	☐	☐	☐	☒	☐

	Never	Rarely	Sometimes	Often	Always
	1	2	3	4	5
21. I am at my best when leading and shepherding a small group of believers.	☐	☐	☑	☐	☐
22. I have strong insight into the Bible and how it applies to people's lives.	☐	☐	☑	☐	☐
23. I feel significant when developing budgets to accomplish a good plan.	☐	☐	☐	☐	☐
24. I am motivated to minister in places where no one else has ministered.	☐	☐	☑	☐	☐
25. I find that unsaved people enjoy spending time with me.	☐	☐	☐	☐	☐
26. I have a strong desire to encourage Christians to mature in Christ.	☐	☐	☐	☐	☐
27. I delight in the truth that God accomplishes things that seem impossible to most people.	☐	☐	☐	☐	☐
28. God has greatly blessed me with life's provisions in order to help others.	☐	☐	☐	☐	☐
29. I enjoy making personal sacrifices to help others.	☐	☐	☐	☐	☐
30. I prefer to lead people more than to follow them.	☐	☐	☐	☐	☐
31. I delight in extending a hand to those in difficulty.	☐	☐	☐	☐	☐
32. I enjoy showing attention to those who are in need of care and concern.	☐	☐	☐	☐	☐
33. I am motivated to present God's truth to people so that they better understand the Bible.	☐	☐	☐	☐	☐
34. I am at my best when creating an organizational structure for a plan.	☐	☐	☐	☐	☐
35. I am definitely a self-starter with a pioneer spirit.	☐	☐	☐	☐	☐
36. I derive extreme satisfaction when lost people accept Christ.	☐	☐	☐	☐	☐

	Never	Rarely	Sometimes	Often	Always
	1	2	3	4	5

37. I have been effective at inspiring believers to a stronger faith. ☐ ☐ ☐ ☐ ☐

38. I am convinced that God is going to accomplish something special through me or my ministry. ☐ ☐ ☐ ☐ ☐

39. I am convinced that all I have belongs to God, and I am willing to use it for his purposes. ☐ ☐ ☐ ☐ ☐

40. I work best when I serve others behind the scenes. ☐ ☐ ☐ ☐ ☐

41. If I am not careful, I have a tendency to dominate people and situations. ☐ ☐ ☐ ☐ ☐

42. I am a born burden-bearer. ☐ ☐ ☐ ☐ ☐

43. I have a deep desire to protect Christians from people and beliefs that may harm them. ☐ ☐ ☐ ☐ ☐

44. I am deeply committed to biblical truth and people's need to know and understand it. ☐ ☐ ☐ ☐ ☐

45. I delight in staffing a particular ministry structure. ☐ ☐ ☐ ☐ ☐

46. I am challenged by a big vision to accomplish what some believe is impossible. ☐ ☐ ☐ ☐ ☐

47. I feel a deep compassion for people who are without Christ. ☐ ☐ ☐ ☐ ☐

48. I have the ability to say the right things to people who are experiencing discouragement. ☐ ☐ ☐ ☐ ☐

49. I am rarely surprised when God turns seeming obstacles into opportunities for ministry. ☐ ☐ ☐ ☐ ☐

50. I feel good when I have opportunity to give from my abundance to people with genuine needs. ☐ ☐ ☐ ☐ ☐

51. I have a strong capacity to serve people. ☐ ☐ ☐ ☐ ☐

52. I am motivated to be proactive, not passive, in my ministry for Christ. ☐ ☐ ☐ ☐ ☐

	Never	Rarely	Sometimes	Often	Always
	1	2	3	4	5
53. I have the ability to feel the pain of others who are suffering.	☐	☐	☐	☐	☐
54. I get excited about helping new Christians grow to maturity in Christ.	☐	☐	☐	☐	☐
55. Whenever I teach a Bible class, the size of the group increases in number.	☐	☐	☐	☐	☐
56. I am good at using a ministry's resources in solving its problems.	☐	☐	☐	☐	☐
57. I gain deep satisfaction from creating something out of nothing.	☐	☐	☐	☐	☐
58. Training and helping others to share their faith is high on my list of priorities.	☐	☐	☐	☐	☐
59. People who are struggling emotionally or spiritually say I am an excellent listener.	☐	☐	☐	☐	☐
60. I delight in trusting God in the most difficult of circumstances.	☐	☐	☐	☐	☐
61. I have the capacity to give of myself as well as my possessions to help others.	☐	☐	☐	☐	☐
62. I am good at doing seemingly insignificant tasks to free people up for vital ministries.	☐	☐	☐	☐	☐
63. Most people place a lot of trust in me and my leadership.	☐	☐	☐	☐	☐
64. I have a desire to make a significant difference in the lives of troubled people.	☐	☐	☐	☐	☐
65. I enjoy being around believers and encouraging them to trust Christ for their circumstances.	☐	☐	☐	☐	☐
66. I have a desire to search the Bible for truths that apply to my life and the lives of others.	☐	☐	☐	☐	☐
67. I like monitoring plans that accomplish ministry goals.	☐	☐	☐	☐	☐
68. I am a risk-taker when it comes to developing new ministries.	☐	☐	☐	☐	☐

	Never	Rarely	Sometimes	Often	Always
	1	2	3	4	5
69. Over the years I have prayed much for my non-Christian friends.	☐	☐	☐	☐	☐
70. I spend a significant amount of time exhorting believers to make Christ Lord of their lives.	☐	☐	☐	☐	☐
71. I am able to trust God in situations when most others have lost all hope.	☐	☐	☐	☐	☐
72. Friends worry that some people take advantage of my generosity with my possessions.	☐	☐	☐	☐	☐
73. I am motivated to accomplish tasks that most people consider insignificant.	☐	☐	☐	☐	☐
74. People are confident in my abilities to help them accomplish their ministry goals.	☐	☐	☐	☐	☐
75. Suffering people are attracted to me and find me comforting to be around.	☐	☐	☐	☐	☐
76. I have the ability and courage to confront Christians about sin in their lives.	☐	☐	☐	☐	☐
77. God has given me unusual ability to explain deep biblical truths to his people.	☐	☐	☐	☐	☐
78. I prefer that a ministry's affairs be conducted in an orderly and efficient manner.	☐	☐	☐	☐	☐
79. I want to accomplish great things for God but in my own way.	☐	☐	☐	☐	☐
80. I am deeply motivated to address the doubts and questions of lost people.	☐	☐	☐	☐	☐
81. I have the ability to confront disobedient Christians and see them change.	☐	☐	☐	☐	☐
82. I am motivated by people who dream big dreams for God.	☐	☐	☐	☐	☐
83. People regularly come to me with requests for help in meeting their financial needs.	☐	☐	☐	☐	☐
84. I look for opportunities to serve the practical needs of God's ministries.	☐	☐	☐	☐	☐

	Never	Rarely	Sometimes	Often	Always
	1	2	3	4	5

85. I am happiest in a ministry when I am able to exert a strong influence in the group. ☐ ☐ ☐ ☐ ☐

86. People close to me believe that I allow "down and outers" to take advantage of me. ☐ ☐ ☐ ☐ ☐

87. Christians often seek me out for counsel regarding important decisions in their lives. ☐ ☐ ☐ ☐ ☐

88. I have a strong desire to study and explain the truths of the Bible in depth. ☐ ☐ ☐ ☐ ☐

89. I am convinced that paying attention to details is very important. ☐ ☐ ☐ ☐ ☐

90. I believe we must create new ministry structures for the new ministries we start. ☐ ☐ ☐ ☐ ☐

91. I feel a strong attraction toward evangelistic ministries. ☐ ☐ ☐ ☐ ☐

92. I could easily spend much of my time encouraging people in their walk with Christ. ☐ ☐ ☐ ☐ ☐

93. I am frustrated by people who never take risks. ☐ ☐ ☐ ☐ ☐

94. I find it difficult to understand why Christians do not give more help to those with real needs. ☐ ☐ ☐ ☐ ☐

95. I prefer to remain behind the scenes helping people with practical matters. ☐ ☐ ☐ ☐ ☐

96. I have a strong desire to take charge in most situations. ☐ ☐ ☐ ☐ ☐

97. I delight in visiting people in hospitals or nursing homes. ☐ ☐ ☐ ☐ ☐

98. I pray constantly for people who look to me for care. ☐ ☐ ☐ ☐ ☐

99. I have observed that people who sit under my teaching experience changed lives. ☐ ☐ ☐ ☐ ☐

100. I have a strong desire to see people work together to accomplish their goals. ☐ ☐ ☐ ☐ ☐

	Never	Rarely	Sometimes	Often	Always
	1	2	3	4	5
101. I am convinced that the future of any country lies in starting fresh ministries.	☐	☐	☐	☐	☐
102. I get extremely frustrated when I cannot share my faith.	☐	☐	☐	☐	☐
103. I find great satisfaction in reassuring Christians of their need to walk with Christ.	☐	☐	☐	☐	☐
104. People are amazed at my ability to trust God to provide in the most difficult situations.	☐	☐	☐	☐	☐
105. When I give significantly to help others, I do not expect anything in return.	☐	☐	☐	☐	☐
106. I am convinced that no job is too menial if it truly helps people.	☐	☐	☐	☐	☐
107. In meetings, people look to me for the final opinion regarding a matter.	☐	☐	☐	☐	☐
108. I believe strongly in giving those who fail a second and even a third chance.	☐	☐	☐	☐	☐
109. I enjoy visiting people in their homes and when they are in the hospital.	☐	☐	☐	☐	☐
110. I am greatly challenged by people's questions about the Bible.	☐	☐	☐	☐	☐

Instructions for Scoring

1. Place the number from each of your answers on the line corresponding to the question number.

2. Add the numbers horizontally and place the total for each row in the space before each gift.

1.__ 12.__ 23.__ 34.__ 45.__ 56.__ 67.__ 78.__ 89.__ 100.__　　___Administration

2.__ 13.__ 24.__ 35.__ 46.__ 57.__ 68.__ 79.__ 90.__ 101.__　　___Apostleship

3.__ 14.__ 25.__ 36.__ 47.__ 58.__ 69.__ 80.__ 91.__ 102.__　　___Evangelism

4.__ 15.__ 26.__ 37.__ 48.__ 59.__ 70.__ 81.__ 92.__ 103.__   ___Encouragement

5.__ 16.__ 27.__ 38.__ 49.__ 60.__ 71.__ 82.__ 93.__ 104.__   ___Faith

6.__ 17.__ 28.__ 39.__ 50.__ 61.__ 72.__ 83.__ 94.__ 105.__   ___Giving

7.__ 18.__ 29.__ 40.__ 51.__ 62.__ 73.__ 84.__ 95.__ 106.__   ___Helps

8.__ 19.__ 30.__ 41.__ 52.__ 63.__ 74.__ 85.__ 96.__ 107.__   ___Leadership

9.__ 20.__ 31.__ 42.__ 53.__ 64.__ 75.__ 86.__ 97.__ 108.__   ___Mercy

10.__ 21.__ 32.__ 43.__ 54.__ 65.__ 76.__ 87.__ 98.__ 109.__   ___Pastor

11.__ 22.__ 33.__ 44.__ 55.__ 66.__ 77.__ 88.__ 99.__ 110.__   ___Teacher

Instructions for Determining Your Spiritual Gifts

1. Place the names of your five highest scoring gifts in the spaces below under Spiritual Gifts Inventory.

2. Place the names of any other gifts that are not identified in this inventory yet are present in your life under the title Other Spiritual Gifts.

Spiritual Gifts Inventory   Other Spiritual Gifts

1._____   _____

2._____   _____

3._____   _____

4._____   _____

5._____   _____

Instructions for Determining
Your Gift-Mix and Gift-Cluster

1. To determine your gift-mix, place the names of your five highest gifts in descending order in the space below titled Gift-Mix.

2. To determine if you have a gift-cluster, decide if the first gift or another gift in your mix is dominant and supported by the other gifts. If this is the case, place it in the center space under the title Gift-Cluster and place the other gifts in the spaces surrounding it.

Gift-Mix

1._____

2._____

3._____

4._____

5._____

Gift-Cluster

_____   _____

_____

_____   _____

Appendix *B*

Temperament Indicator 1

Instructions

Read the four terms listed across each line. Then rank each characteristic for how well it describes you in a ministry or work-related environment. Number 4 is most like you, and number 1 is least. Each word will have a number 1, 2, 3, or 4.

Sample: _3_ Direct   _4_ Popular   _1_ Loyal   _2_ Analytical

___Decisive   ___Outgoing   ___Dependable   ___Logical

___Controlling   ___Expressive   ___Steady   ___Thorough

___Competent   ___Influential   ___Responsible   ___Skeptical

___Blunt   ___Enthusiastic   ___Sensible   ___Compliant

___Competitive   ___Persuasive   ___Cooperative   ___Serious

___Callous   ___Impulsive   ___Submissive   ___Accurate

___Volatile   ___Manipulative   ___Conforming   ___Picky

___Persistent   ___Personable   ___Harmonious   ___Creative

___Productive   ___Animated   ___Restrained   ___Fearful

___Self-reliant   ___Articulate   ___Predictable   ___Diplomatic

___*Total*   ___*Total*   ___*Total*   ___*Total*

Instructions for Scoring

1. Total the numbers in each column above and place that number in the blank provided at the bottom of each column.
2. On the scale below, circle the number in each column that is closest to the total score for the above column.
3. Connect the circles.
4. The highest number represents your strongest temperament type. The next highest represents your second strongest temperament type.
5. Have someone who knows you well complete the indicator on you. Compare the scores and discuss any differences.

50	50	50	50
45	45	45	45
40	40	40	40
35	35	35	35
30	30	30	30
25	25	25	25
20	20	20	20
15	15	15	15
10	10	10	10
5	5	5	5
0	0	0	0
Doer	**Influencer**	**Relator**	**Thinker**

Temperament Indicator 2

Instructions

1. As you take this indicator, please keep in mind that there are no correct or incorrect answers.

2. Read each statement and circle the item (a or b)that best represents your preference in a ministry or work-related environment.

3. Do not spend a lot of time thinking over your answers. Go with your first impulse.

Questions

1. When around other people, I am
   a) expressive
   b) quiet

2. I tend to
   a) dislike new problems
   b) like new problems

3. I make decisions based on my
   a) logic
   b) values

4. I prefer to work in a
   a) structured environment
   b) nonstructured environment

5. I feel more energetic after being
   a) around people
   b) away from people

6. I work best with
   a) facts
   b) ideas

7. People say I am
   a) impersonal
   b) a people-pleaser

8. My friends at work say I am very
   a) organized
   b) flexible

9. I get more work accomplished when I am
   a) with people
   b) by myself

10. I like to think about
    a) what is
    b) what could be

11. I admire
    a) strength
    b) compassion

12. I make decisions
    a) quickly
    b) slowly

13. I prefer
    a) variety and action
    b) focus and quiet

14. I like
    a) established ways to do things
    b) new ways to do things

15. I tend to be rather
    a) unemotional
    b) emotional

16. Most often I dislike
    a) carelessness with details
    b) complicated procedures

17. In my relationships I find that over time it is easy to
    a) keep up with people
    b) lose track of people

18. I enjoy skills that
    a) I have already learned and used
    b) are newly learned but unused

19. Sometimes I make decisions that
    a) hurt other people's feelings
    b) are too influenced by other people

20. When my circumstances change, I prefer to
    a) follow a good plan
    b) adapt to each new situation

21. In conversations I communicate
    a) freely and openly
    b) quietly and cautiously

22. In my work I tend to
    a) take time to be precise
    b) dislike taking time to be precise

23. I relate well to
    a) people like me
    b) most people

24. When working on a project, I do not
    a) like interruptions
    b) mind interruptions

25. Sometimes I find that I
    a) act first and ask questions later
    b) ask questions first and act later

26. I would describe my work style as
    a) steady with realistic expectations
    b) periodic with bursts of enthusiasm

27. At work I need
    a) fair treatment
    b) occasional praise

28. In a new job I prefer to know
    a) only what it takes to get it done
    b) all about it

29. In any job I am most interested in
    a) getting it done and the results
    b) the idea behind the job

30. I have found that I am
    a) patient with routine details
    b) impatient with routine details

31. When working with other people, I find it
    a) easy to correct them
    b) difficult to correct them

32. Once I have made a decision, I consider the case
    a) closed
    b) still open

33. I prefer
    a) lots of acquaintances
    b) a few good friends

34. I am more likely to trust my
    a) experiences
    b) inspirations

35. I consistently decide matters based on
    a) the facts in my head
    b) the feelings in my heart

36. I prefer to work
    a) in an established business
    b) as an entrepreneur

Instructions for Scoring

1. Place a check in the a or b box below to indicate how you answered each question.
2. Add the checks down each column and record the total for each column at the bottom.
3. The highest score for each pair indicates your temperament preference.
4. For each pair subtract the lower from the higher score to discover the difference in your preferences. A higher number indicates a clear choice or preference but does not indicate the measure of development. For example, a higher score for extraversion means

that you prefer it over introversion. It does not mean that you are a strong extravert.

	a	b		a	b		a	b		a	b
1	__	__	2	__	__	3	__	__	4	__	__
5	__	__	6	__	__	7	__	__	8	__	__
9	__	__	10	__	__	11	__	__	12	__	__
13	__	__	14	__	__	15	__	__	16	__	__
17	__	__	18	__	__	19	__	__	20	__	__
21	__	__	22	__	__	23	__	__	24	__	__
25	__	__	26	__	__	27	__	__	28	__	__
29	__	__	30	__	__	31	__	__	32	__	__
33	__	__	34	__	__	35	__	__	36	__	__
Total	__	__	**Total**	__	__	**Total**	__	__	**Total**	__	__
	E	**I**		**S**	**N**		**T**	**F**		**J**	**P**
	Extravert	Introvert		Sensing	Intuition		Thinking	Feeling		Judgment	Perception

Leadership Role Indicator

Instructions

1. There are no correct or incorrect answers to the questions.

2. Read each statement carefully and circle the item (a, b, or c) that *best* represents your leadership role. Do not be too quick to circle item c (both).

3. Do not spend too much time with each question; instead go with your initial impulse.

Questions

1. In my approach to change, I
   a) cope with change
   b) cope with complexity
   c) both

2. In leading an organization or ministry, I
   a) do the right things
   b) do things right
   c) both

3. When viewing my work or ministry, I see
   a) the whole
   b) the parts
   c) both

4. My general outlook on life and ministry is
    a) optimistic
    b) realistic
    c) both

5. In my work or ministry, I operate on the basis of
    a) faith
    b) facts
    c) both

6. In my role as a leader, I might be described as
    a) an influencer
    b) a coordinator
    c) both

7. When I view my work or ministry, I think in terms of
    a) opportunity
    b) accomplishment
    c) both

8. In my work or ministry, I seek
    a) effectiveness
    b) efficiency
    c) both

9. In my leadership, I would describe myself as a
    a) visionary
    b) realist
    c) both

10. In my work or ministry, my focus is on
    a) ideas
    b) functions
    c) both

11. In my work or ministry, I can be counted on to provide
    a) direction
    b) control
    c) both

12. In my leadership role, I see myself as
    a) a persuader
    b) an implementer
    c) both

13. In my work or ministry, I would describe myself as a
    a) risk-taker
    b) stabilizer
    c) both

14. When communicating to a group, people say that I speak
    a) persuasively
    b) informationally
    c) both

15. One of my desires for my job or ministry is to see
    a) growth
    b) harmony
    c) both

16. I tend to think
    a) inductively
    b) deductively
    c) both

17. I have the spiritual gift(s) of
    a) leadership
    b) administration
    c) both

18. In my work or ministry, I am
    a) proactive
    b) reactive
    c) both

Instructions for Scoring

1. Place a check in the a, b, or c spaces below to indicate how you answered each question.

2. Add the checks down each column and record the totals for each column at the bottom.

3. The highest column score indicates your leadership role.

	a	b	c
1	___	___	___
2	___	___	___
3	___	___	___
4	___	___	___
5	___	___	___
6	___	___	___
7	___	___	___
8	___	___	___
9	___	___	___
10	___	___	___
11	___	___	___
12	___	___	___
13	___	___	___
14	___	___	___
15	___	___	___
16	___	___	___
17	___	___	___
18	___	___	___
Total	___	___	___
	Leader	Manager	Both

Natural Gifts and Talents Inventory

Instructions

1. Look over the following list of potential church and parachurch ministries. Circle any you have enjoyed doing in the past or think you might enjoy doing in the future.

2. For each circled item, indicate the degree of your interest by placing a letter in front of it from the following scale:

A. Passionate interest
B. Strong interest
C. Slight interest

___ accounting	___ building and grounds
___ administration	___ children
___ adolescents	___ coaching
___ advertising and publicity	___ cooking
___ adults	___ custodial
___ art	___ directing traffic
___ audiovisual	___ drama
___ bookkeeping	___ evangelism

___ facilities maintenance   ___ preaching

___ finances   ___ shepherding

___ graphic design   ___ singing

___ greeting   ___ small groups

___ helps   ___ sound control

___ hospitality   ___ stage production

___ leadership   ___ teaching

___ lighting   ___ telephoning

___ library   ___ typing

___ marketing   ___ visitation

___ ministry assessment   ___ word processing

___ parking   ___ worship

___ playing a musical instrument   ___ writing

Appendix F

Natural Gifts and Abilities Indicator

Instructions

1. Look over the following list of occupations and vocational topics. Circle any you have enjoyed doing in the past or think you would enjoy pursuing in the future.

2. For each circled item, indicate the degree of your interest by placing a letter in front of it from the following scale:

A. Passionate interest
B. Strong interest
C. Slight interest

Vocational Topics

___ accounting

___ advertising

___ agriculture

___ architecture

___ armed services

___ art

___ automotive services

___ business

___ computer science

___ cooking

___ electronics

___ engineering

___ industrial arts

___ insurance

___ law enforcement

___ management

___ marketing

___ mathematics

___ medicine

___ ministry

___ music

___ politics

___ psychology

___ psychiatry

___ real estate

___ sales

___ science

___ social work

___ teaching

___ theater

Occupations

___ actor/actress

___ accountant

___ appraiser

___ architect

___ artist

___ athlete

___ carpenter

___ chef

___ coach

___ comedian

___ computer specialist

___ construction worker

___ contractor

___ counselor

___ dancer

___ designer

___ mathematician

___ mechanic

___ minister

___ musician

___ nurse

___ nutritionist

___ physician

___ physical therapist

___ pilot

___ policeman

___ politician

___ professor

___ psychiatrist

___ psychologist

___ realtor

___ reporter

___ detective

___ driver

___ economist

___ electrician

___ engineer

___ entertainer

___ farmer

___ hair specialist

___ homemaker

___ inventor

___ investor

___ marketer

___ sailor

___ salesperson

___ secretary

___ schoolteacher

___ soldier

___ singer

___ social worker

___ stockbroker

___ scientist

___ welder

___ writer

Spiritual Gifts Inventories

Inventories That Include Sign Gifts

Wagner-Modified Houts Questionnaire
Charles E. Fuller Institute
P.O. Box 91990
Pasadena, CA 91109–1990

Wesley Spiritual Gifts Questionnaire
Charles E. Fuller Institute
P.O. Box 91990
Pasadena, CA 91109–1990

Inventories That Exclude Sign Gifts

Discover Your Gifts
Church Development Resources
2850 Kalamazoo Avenue
Grand Rapids, MI 49560

Houts Inventory of Spiritual Gifts
Charles E. Fuller Institute
P.O. Box 91990
Pasadena, CA 91109–1990

Spiritual Gifts Analysis
McCart Meadows Baptist Church
2729 Sagehill Drive
Fort Worth, TX 76123

Spiritual Gifts Inventory Questionnaire
Church Growth Institute
P.O. Box 4404
Lynchburg, VA 24502

Trenton Spiritual Gifts Analysis
Charles E. Fuller Institute
P.O. Box 91990
Pasadena, CA 91109–1990

Appendix H

Assessment Organizations

The Doma Group
P.O. Box 1278
Burnsville, MN 55337
(612) 895–1544

Network Ministries International
27355 Betanzos
Mission Viejo, CA 92692
(800) 588–8833

The Profile Group, Inc.
17822 East Lehigh Place
Aurora, CO 80013
(303) 693–7492

Vision Ministries International
5041 Urban Crest
Dallas, TX 75227
(214) 841–3777

Notes

Chapter 1

1. Ralph Mattson and Arthur Miller, *Finding a Job You Can Love* (Nashville: Thomas Nelson Publishers, 1982), 123.

2. Ibid.

3. A variety of models exist as based on the physiological, cognitive, behavioral, psychoanalytic, humanistic, or genetic perspectives of psychology. See Rod Plotnik and Sandra Mollenauer, *Introduction to Psychology* (New York: Random House, 1986), 5–10. The deterministic model is often referred to today as the behavioral model; the developmental as the humanist model.

4. See the brief discussion on this in Gerald Corey, *Theory and Practice of Counseling and Psychotherapy,* 4th ed. (Pacific Grove, Calif.: Brooks/Cole Publishing Company, 1991), 293.

5. Whereas Skinner ruled out the possibility of any self-determination and freedom, the current trend allows that an individual has some ability to choose.

6. Plotnik and Mollenauer, *Introduction to Psychology,* 9.

7. Mattson and Miller, *Finding a Job You Can Love,* 123.

8. Lyle Schaller, *Activating the Passive Church: Diagnosis and Treatment* (Nashville: Abingdon Press, 1981), 11.

9. Source unknown.

10. In Frank Tillapaugh's *Unleashing the Church* (Ventura, Calif.: Regal, 1982), 20.

Chapter 2

1. Every Christian should explore both his dignity and his depravity in that order. We are able to deal with our depravity best when we consider it in the context of our dignity. To focus on one without considering the other leads to an extreme. For example, to focus on our depravity alone, as Christians are prone to do, results in a low view of ourselves that is not biblical and leads to discouragement, depression, and low self-esteem. To focus only on our dignity can produce spiritual pride.

2. A part of knowing who we are includes all that has taken place spiritually as the result of being in Christ. This includes such divine blessings as forgiveness, redemption, reconciliation, justification, propitiation, and many others. This topic is most important and is covered in other books such as Lewis Sperry Chafer, *Systematic Theology*, vol. 2, ch. 4 (abridged edition); Robert S. McGee, *The Search for Significance*, chs. 6–9; and Neil Anderson, *Victory over the Darkness*, chs. 1–3. Because these books cover this topic so well, I have chosen not to repeat it in this book.

3. I first heard this from Bruce Bugbee who is the founder and president of Network Ministries International, which provides training and support for volunteer and staff identification and placement according to one's divine design. This excellent organization also provides tapes, seminars, and written materials as well as comprehensive training through Networking University. For more information see appendix H.

4. Mattson and Miller, *Finding a Job You Can Love*, 119.

5. The idea of using the term *limitations* here rather than *weaknesses* is the idea of Dr. William Lawrence, the executive director of the Center for Christian Leadership at Dallas Theological Seminary.

6. Donald A. McGavran, *Understanding Church Growth* (Grand Rapids: Eerdmans, 1970), 223.

7. For further discussion of the homogeneous principle see Aubrey Malphurs, *Planting Growing Churches for the 21st Century* (Grand Rapids: Baker Book House, 1992), 168–71.

8. A definition used by Brad Smith in a brochure for the Center for Christian Leadership on the theme of authenticity published by Dallas Theological Seminary, Summer 1992.

9. A definition used by Dr. William Lawrence in a paper presented to the National Association of Professors of Christian Education entitled "Vision for Personal and Leadership Development," October 1992, 9.

10. Ibid.

11. An excellent book that is designed to help teams function well together is Glenn Parker's *Team Players and Teamwork* (San Francisco: Jossey-Bass Publishers, 1990).

Chapter 3

1. Charles C. Ryrie, *The Holy Spirit* (Chicago: Moody Press, 1965), 83.

2. Each question is preceded by a negative Greek particle that implies that the expected answer is no. See H. E. Dana and Julius R. Mantey, *A Manual Grammar of the Greek New Testament* (New York: Macmillan, 1955), 265.

3. Robert Clinton, *The Making of a Leader* (Colorado Springs: Navpress, 1988), 92.

4. Bruce Bugbee, an assistant pastor at Willow Creek Community Church near Chicago, includes the gifts of counseling, craftsmanship, and creative communica-

tion in his list of gifts. Bruce L. Bugbee, *Networking: Participants Manual* (The Charles E. Fuller Institute of Evangelism and Church Growth, P.O. Box 91990, Pasadena, CA 91109–1990), 51.

5. Some argue that these gifts were limited in their use to the first century during the foundational period of the church. See William McRae, *The Dynamics of Spiritual Gifts* (Grand Rapids: Zondervan Publishing House, 1976), 64–75, 90–99; and Joseph C. Dillow, *Speaking in Tongues* (Grand Rapids: Zondervan Publishing House, 1975).

6. See my thesis for the Department of New Testament Literature and Exegesis, "The Relationship of Pastors and Teachers in Ephesians 4:11" (Th.M. thesis, Dallas Theological Seminary, 1978).

7. Kevin W. McCarthy, *The On-Purpose Person* (Colorado Springs: Pinion Press, 1992), 108.

8. Bill Hybels, *Honest to God?* (Grand Rapids: Zondervan Publishing House, 1990), 112.

9. Fergus P. Hughes and Lloyd D. Noppe, *Human Development: Across the Life Span* (St. Paul, Minn.: West Publishing Company, 1985), 378.

10. Ibid.

11. James C. Dobson, *Parenting Isn't for Cowards* (Waco, Tex.: Word Publishing, 1987), 24.

12. Ken Voges and Ron Braund, *Understanding How Others Misunderstand You* (Chicago: Moody Press, 1990), 39.

13. I develop these preferences in more detail in chapter 4.

14. Hybels, *Honest to God?*, 114.

15. Ibid., 73.

16. As Christians, we must not forget that many people who may not profess Christ are just as concerned with accuracy and arriving at truth as we are.

17. Sylvan J. Kaplan and Barbara E. W. Kaplan, *The Kaplan Report: A Study of the Validity of the Personal Profile System* (Chevy Chase, Md.: Performax Systems, Inc., 1983).

18. Isabel Briggs Myers and Mary H. McCaulley, *Manual: A Guide to the Development and Use of the Myers-Briggs Type Indicator* (Palo Alto, Calif.: Consulting Psychologists Press, 1985), ch. 11.

19. Roland Kenneth Harrison, *Introduction to the Old Testament* (Grand Rapids: Eerdmans, 1969), 1004.

20. Ibid., 1007–8.

21. Ibid., 1006.

22. Ibid., 1007.

23. Derek Kidner, *Proverbs: An Introduction and Commentary* (Downers Grove, Ill.: InterVarsity Press, 1964), 17.

24. David Ward, "Theologically Justifying Personality Type Training," a student paper presented at Dallas Theological Seminary, Dallas, Texas, 1992, 3.

25. Mels Carbonell covers nine spiritual gifts and how they combine with the D, I, S, and C temperaments in his booklet *Uniquely You in Christ: Combination—Personalities and Spiritual Gifts Profile.* You may purchase this tool by writing to the following address: 255 Bellevue Loop, Fayetteville, GA 30214, or calling (404) 461–4243.

26. While some distinctions probably exist between management and administration depending on the area of study (education, military, government, or business), for purposes of simplicity, this book will treat them as fundamentally the same.

27. John P. Kotter, "What Leaders Really Do," *Harvard Business Review*, May–June 1990, 103.

28. See the following on leadership: Ted W. Engstrom, *The Making of a Christian Leader* (Grand Rapids: Zondervan Publishing House, 1976), 23; Abraham Zaleznik, "Managers and Leaders: Are They Different?" *Harvard Business Review*, May–June 1977, 67–78; Bruce W. Jones, *Ministerial Leadership in a Managerial World* (Wheaton, Ill.: Tyndale House Publishers, Inc., 1988), 39–52; Mary E. Tramel and Helen Reynolds, *Executive Leadership* (Englewood Cliffs, N.J.: Prentice-Hall, 1981), 59–60.

29. Kotter, "What Leaders Really Do," 104.

30. Ibid.

31. Warren Bennis and Burt Nanus, *Leaders: The Strategies for Taking Charge* (New York: Harper & Row, 1985), 21.

32. Peter R. Drucker, *The Effective Executive* (New York: Harper & Row, 1967), 4.

33. C. Peter Wagner, *Leading Your Church to Growth* (Ventura, Calif.: Regal, 1984), 89.

34. Ken R. Voges, *Biblical Personal Profile* (Minneapolis: Performax Systems International, 1985), 7.

35. Voges and Braund, *Understanding How Others Misunderstand You,* 70.

36. Jones, *Ministerial Leadership in a Managerial World,* 110.

37. Voges, *Biblical Personal Profile,* 7.

38. Voges and Braund, *Understanding How Others Misunderstand You,* 70.

39. Jones, *Ministerial Leadership in a Managerial World,* 110.

40. Voges, *Biblical Personal Profile,* 7.

41. Voges and Braund, *Understanding How Others Misunderstand You,* 70.

42. Jones, *Ministerial Leadership in a Managerial World,* 110.

43. Voges, *Biblical Personal Profile,* 7.

44. Voges and Braund, *Understanding How Others Misunderstand You,* 70.

45. Jones, *Ministerial Leadership in a Managerial World,* 110.

46. Hybels, *Honest to God?,* 126.

47. Ibid., 127.

48. Ibid., 128–29.

49. Ibid., 129.

50. Ibid., 130.

51. Ibid., 131.

52. Ibid.

53. Ibid., 132.

54. Exploring these in more detail is beyond the purpose of this book. However, if you desire to pursue your design in any of these areas, several of the articles I have cited in the footnotes contain quizzes and explanations.

55. Mattson and Miller, *Finding a Job You Can Love,* 98–99.

56. Penny Zeitler, "Not Everyone Learns Alike," *Leadership,* Summer 1987, 28–33. See also Bernice McCarthy, *The 4MAT System,* EXCEL, Inc., 200 West Station Street, Barrington, IL 60010.

57. Knowing our learning style can be very useful. Students could decide on class projects and select their teachers based on learning style. Teachers could base their instructional methodology as well as their assignments on their students' learning styles.

58. Norman Shawchuck, *How to Manage Conflict in the Church: Understanding and Managing Conflict* (Glendale Heights, Ill.: Spiritual Growth Resources, 1983), 23–27.

59. Robert M. Bramson and Susan Bramson, "What Kind of Thinker Are You?" *Reader's Digest,* December 1987, 149–52.

60. Glenn M. Parker, *Team Players and Teamwork* (San Francisco: Jossey-Bass Publishers, 1990), ch. 3.

61. Parker includes a survey on pages 159–64 to help you determine your team-player style.

Chapter 4

1. William McRae, *The Dynamics of Spiritual Gifts* (Grand Rapids: Zondervan Publishing House, 1976), 114.

2. This inventory does not include all the gifts such as the sign gifts. If you desire to be tested for the sign gifts as well, then take one of the appropriate inventories in appendix G.

3. J. Robert Clinton, *The Making of a Leader* (Colorado Springs: NavPress, 1988), 92.

4. Ibid.

5. Ibid.

6. I have designed these two instruments specifically for this book. They are aids only to help you get started in the discovery process. You should follow these with the other, more sophisticated instruments of high validity.

7. You can purchase both profiles from the Charles E. Fuller Institute of Evangelism and Church Growth, P.O. Box 91990, Pasadena, CA 91109–1990, (800) 999–9578. You may also be able to purchase them from a counseling organization

in your area. For a name or address contact the Carlson Learning Company, P.O. Box 59159, Minneapolis, MN 55459–8247 or call (612) 449–2856.

8. Bob Phillips, *The Delicate Art of Dancing with Porcupines* (Ventura, Calif.: Regal Books, 1989).

9. For information as to the availability of the MBTI in your area, contact the Center for Applications of Psychological Type, 2815 N.W. 13th Street, Suite 401, Gainesville, FL 32609, (904) 375–0160. This inventory is not available to the general public. You must take it through a professional counseling center, a consulting organization, or the departments of education or psychology at a nearby college or university.

10. The *Keirsey Temperament Sorter* costs only 25 cents. You can order copies from Prometheus Nemesis Book Company, Box 2748, Del Mar, CA 92014 or call (619) 632–1575.

11. David Keirsey and Marilyn Bates, *Please Understand Me* (Del Mar, Calif.: Promethean Books, Inc., 1978).

12. Roy M. Oswald and Otto Kroeger, *Personality Type and Religious Leadership* (Washington, D.C.: The Alban Institute, 1988).

13. Ken R. Voges, *Biblical Personal Profile* (Minneapolis: Performax Systems International, 1985), 21.

14. Ibid.

15. Ibid.

16. I have designed this tool to get you started in the process of determining your leadership role. It has not been validated and may not accurately reflect your leadership role. I am not aware of any other tool that helps determine leadership role, however.

17. Mels Carbonell demonstrates how the gift of evangelism combines with the four temperaments in his booklet, *Uniquely You in Christ: Combination—Personalities and Spiritual Gifts Profile.*

18. You may order this tool from National Computer Systems, Inc., P.O. Box 1294, Minneapolis, MN 55440.

19. Herbert A. Shepard and Jack A. Hawley, *Life Planning: Personal and Organizational* (Washington, D.C.: National Training and Development Service Press, 1974).

20. James M. Kouzes and Barry Z. Posner, *The Leadership Challenge: How to Get Extraordinary Things Done in Organizations* (San Francisco: Jossey-Bass Publishers, 1987), 101.

Chapter 5

1. Frank Tillapaugh, *Unleashing the Church,* 20.

2. Aubrey Malphurs, *Vision America: A Strategy for Reaching a Nation* (Grand Rapids: Baker Book House, 1994), ch. 4.

3. Lyle E. Schaller, *Getting Things Done* (Nashville: Abingdon, 1986), 152–53.

4. Kent and Barbara Hughes, *Liberating Ministry from the Success Syndrome* (Wheaton, Ill.: Tyndale House Publishers, Inc., 1988), 125.

5. Ibid., 126.

6. Ibid.

7. Ibid., 129–31.

8. Arthur J. DeJong, *Reclaiming a Mission* (Grand Rapids: Eerdmans, 1990), 63.

9. In fact, some old paradigm churches are hostile toward them.

10. Jerry White, *The Church and the Parachurch: An Uneasy Marriage* (Portland, Oreg.: Multnomah Press, 1983), 36.

11. Ibid., 54.

12. Leith Anderson, *Dying for Change* (Minneapolis: Bethany House Publishers, 1990), 10.

13. Ibid.

14. White, *The Church and the Parachurch*, 106–10.

15. Ibid., 89–93.

16. William McRae, *The Principles of the New Testament Church* (Dallas: Believers Chapel, 1974), 17.

17. The topic of women serving as pastors and elders is hotly debated among evangelicals today. I believe that 1 Timothy 2:11–15 and 1 Corinthians 11:3 teach that they are not to be in the position of pastor or elder.

Chapter 6

1. For more information see Aubrey Malphurs, *Planting Growing Churches for the 21st Century* (Grand Rapids: Baker Book House, 1992), 152–54.

2. Robert W. Thomas, "Personality Characteristics of Effective Revitalization Pastors in Small, Passive, Baptist General Conference Churches" (D. Min. Dissertation, Talbot School of Theology, 1989), 1. Some might object to his use of trait theory as an approach to assessment. Thomas defends this practice on pages 26–32.

3. Ibid.

4. In chapter 3 we saw that this profile consists of a high I temperament combined with a secondary D. It is a combination of the temperaments of two biblical characters, Peter and Paul.

5. John G. Geier and Dorothy E. Downey, *Personal Profile System* (Minneapolis: Performax Systems International, 1977), 17.

6. In *Pouring New Wine into Old Wineskins: How to Change a Church Without Destroying It* (Grand Rapids: Baker Book House, 1993), ch. 4, I bring other divine design elements to bear on the issue of who makes good renewal pastors.

7. Ken R. Voges, *Workbook: Level 1 Part A*. The Biblical Behavioral Series (Minneapolis: Performax Systems International, 1986), 6. Italics mine.

8. Malphurs, *Planting Growing Churches for the 21st Century*, ch. 6.

9. Ibid., 91.

10. For more information, contact Mr. Paul Williams at P.O. Box 9, East Islip, NY 11730–0009.

11. Malphurs, *Planting Growing Churches for the 21st Century*, 99–100.

12. Thomas, *Personality Characteristics*, 113–14.

13. Paul D. Tieger and Barbara Barron-Tieger, *Do What You Are* (Boston: Little, Brown & Company, 1992), 90.

14. Ibid., 89.

Chapter 7

1. David P. Ludeker, "Training for Ministry: A Life-Time Experience," *American Baptist Quarterly*, June 1984, 116.

2. Lyle E. Schaller, "Megachurch!" *Christianity Today*, March 5, 1990, 23.

3. H. Richard Niebuhr, *The Purpose of the Church and Its Ministry: Reflections on the Aims of Theological Education* (New York: Harper and Brothers, 1956), 107.

4. R. Paul Stevens, "Marketing the Faith—A Reflection on the Importing and Exporting of Western Theological Education," *Crux*, June 1992, 9.

5. There is a tendency for most faculties, at least on the seminary level, to be short on practical experience, especially in the local church. This is not good because these same people have much to say in the design of the school's curriculum that influences future pastors. Seminaries would be wise to require more local church experience of its faculty, in particular those who teach in the language and theology departments.

6. For more information or a catalog, their address is P.O. Box 90095, Pasadena, CA 91109–5095, or call (800) 999–9578.

7. Address: P.O. Box 1012, Littleton, CO 80160. Phone: (303) 798–8102.

Chapter 8

1. This is true of the high D temperament.

2. Norman Shawchuck, *How to Manage Conflict in the Church: Understanding and Managing Conflict* (Glendale Heights, Ill.: Spiritual Growth Resources, 1983), 23–27.

3. In this section on skills, I am including perceptual skills with motor skills, although they may belong to different domains. Cf. Leroy Ford, *A Curriculum Design Manual for Theological Education* (Nashville: Broadman Press, 1991), 89.

Index

Aubrey Malphurs is the president of Vision Ministries International and is available for consultation on various topics related to leadership, vision, church planting, and church renewal. Those wishing to contact him for consulting or speaking engagements may do so through the following:

Vision Ministries International
5041 Urban Crest
Dallas, TX 75227
(214) 841-3777